CONTEMPORARY'S

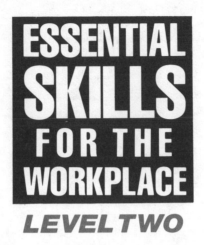

ESSENTIAL SKILLS FOR THE WORKPLACE

LEVEL TWO

Improving Workplace Performance

Series Developer
Lori Strumpf
President, Center for Remediation Design

Author
Beth Blanchard-Smith

Project Editor
Sarah Conroy Williams

CONTEMPORARY
BOOKS

CHICAGO

Library of Congress Cataloging-in-Publication Data

Strumpf, Lori.
    Essential skills for the workplace. Improving Workplace
Performance / Lori Strumpf & Beth Blanchard-Smith.
        p.   cm.
    ISBN 0-8092-3900-0 (paper)
    1. Office practice—Handbooks, manuals, etc.   2. Business—
Forms—Handbooks, manuals, etc.   3. Business records—
Handbooks, manual, etc.   4. Secretaries—Vocational guidance—
Handbooks, manuals, etc.   I. Blanchard-Smith, Beth.   II. Title.
HF5547.5.S8172   1993
651.7—dc20   93-22805
                                                                      CIP

Published by Contemporary Books, Inc.
Two Prudential Plaza, Chicago, Illinois 60601-6790
Manufactured in the United States of America
International Standard Book Number: 0-8092-3900-0
10   9   8   7   6   5   4   3

Published simultaneously in Canada by
Fitzhenry & Whiteside
195 Allstate Parkway
Markham, Ontario L3R 4T8
Canada

Editorial Director	*Editorial Production Manager*	*Typography*
Mark Boone	Norma Underwood	Point West, Inc.
		Carol Stream, Illinois
Executive Editor	*Production Editor*	
Cathy Niemet	Thomas D. Scharf	Special thanks to Caren Van Slyke
Editorial	*Art & Production*	Cover design by Georgene Sainati
Owen Hurd	Todd Petersen	Cover photo © Westlight
Sharon Rundo	Jan Geist	Photo manipulation by
Holly Graskewitz		Kristin Nelson, Provizion
	Illustrator	
Editorial Assistant	Kathy Dzielak	
Maggie McCann		

Photo Credits
Page 5: © Gilles Peress/Magnum Photos, Inc. Page 6: ©
Leonard Freed/Magnum Photos, Inc. Page 23: © Jeff Cadget/
The Image Bank. Page 24: © Janeart Ltd./The Image Bank. Page
30: © Carol Bernson/The Image Bank. Page 37: © Alvis Upitis/
The Image Bank. Page 38: © A. Darazien/The Image Bank. Page
51: © Guido A. Rossi/The Image Bank. Page 52: © P. Markow/
F.P.G. Page 69: © Jay Freis/The Image Bank. Page 70: © Jay
Freis/The Image Bank. Page 70: © Lee Balterman/F.P.G. Page
83: A. McGee/F.P.G. Page 84: © Ralph Brunke. Page 97: © Jay
Freis/The Image Bank. Page 111: Lisa Goodman/The Image
Bank. Page 112: Steve Dunwell/The Image Bank.

Essential Skills for the Workplace stems from a national
demonstration project conducted by the Center for
Remediation Design (CRD), a joint project of the U.S.
Conference of Mayors, the National Association of Private
Industry Councils, the Partnership for Training and
Employment Careers, and the National Association of
Counties. The CRD's primary goal is to help employers
and training providers link basic skills training to the needs
of the workplace.

The Project of the States, conducted by the CRD, the
Center for Human Resources at Brandeis University, and
select JTPA entities since 1987, focuses on the use of
reading, writing, computation, problem solving, and
communication skills in the workplace. Competencies
singled out by this project's labor market studies as being
essential to a successful workforce are the foundation for
the lessons in this series.

CONTENTS

ACKNOWLEDGMENTS

Medical forms on pages 12, 19, and 145 used by permission of Inpatient Nursing, St. John's Health System, Anderson, Indiana.

Travel information on pages 57, 58, and 161 from *Frommer's Hawaii '92*, by Faye Hammel, © 1992. Used by permission of Prentice Hall General Reference, a division of Simon & Schuster, New York.

Cash register keyboard on page 108 used by permission of Sharp Electronics Corporation.

Airline information on page 159 used by permission of *Official Airline Guides*. All rights reserved.

Panasonic vacuum information on page 169 used by permission of Matsushita Electric Corporation of America.

Riccar vacuum information on page 169 used by permission of Riccar America.

TO THE LEARNER

Contemporary's *Essential Skills for the Workplace* series has four books—two books in Level One, two books in Level Two. Each book integrates, or combines, the reading, math, writing, communication, and problem-solving skills you need to complete tasks at the workplace and in everyday life.

Essential Skills for the Workplace will take you out of the classroom and into the world of work. Each task in these books is a task you may encounter in the workplace. In addition, each task is part of the "big picture"—part of the process required to make a business purchase, for example, or to prepare a business delivery.

This book, *Improving Workplace Performance*, is part of Level Two of the series. In this book you'll complete tasks you would perform in each of the eight career areas presented. The three Units in each book are separated according to the level of difficulty. The tasks become more complex in Units II and III. When you finish the two workbooks in Level Two, you will have learned important skills needed to function well in the workplace.

In Level Two, you will

- ▶ visualize the steps you need to take to complete a task from start to finish
- ▶ prioritize tasks and do them in the order in which you would complete them
- ▶ make notes to help you organize your thoughts
- ▶ recap each task to check if you followed all the necessary steps
- ▶ review your plan to see if you might have done anything differently
- ▶ use the skills you've learned in your everyday life

Skills addressed in Level Two are:

- ▶ selecting resources (time, money, materials, space, and staff)
- ▶ gathering and interpreting information
- ▶ learning about organizational systems
- ▶ practicing interpersonal communication
- ▶ selecting technology and tools

In the back of the book, you'll find an answer key and a glossary of workplace terms. The words in boldface type throughout the book are the words defined in the glossary. You will also find several resource pages you'll need to complete the various workplace tasks.

We hope you enjoy *Essential Skills for the Workplace Level Two: Improving Workplace Performance*. We wish you the best of luck in your studies.

The Editors

■■■ HEALTHCARE

The healthcare industry is one of the fastest-growing fields in the United States. Nearly 4 million jobs are expected to open in the health services industry by the year 2005. More and more health service workers will be needed to care for the growing number of elderly Americans. Advances in medical technology also require more workers in new types of health services. Workers in this field care for others. They help people improve their physical well-being.

SOME SKILLS YOU WILL PRACTICE IN THIS LESSON

▶ Adjust a Schedule
▶ Prioritize Information
▶ Plan an Exam Procedure
▶ Build a Team
▶ Update a Record

One job in the growing healthcare field is medical assistant. These assistants help physicians examine and treat patients. They perform both clinical and administrative tasks.

Medical assistants take and record patients' medical histories. They prepare patients for exams and collect samples of blood or urine. They also schedule appointments and fill out and file patients' records. Most medical assistants work in doctors' offices, but a growing number work in clinics and hospitals.

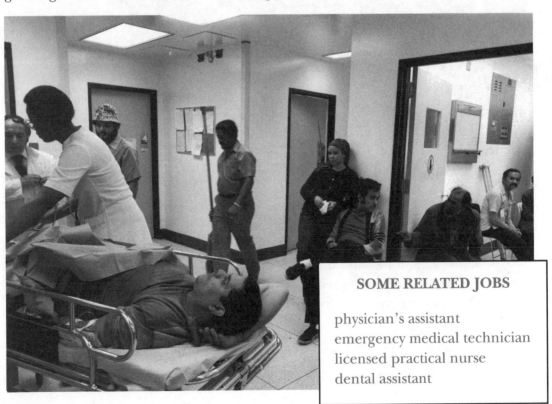

SOME RELATED JOBS

physician's assistant
emergency medical technician
licensed practical nurse
dental assistant

All in a Day's Work

You've had a busy morning in your job as a medical assistant.

As you walk by the front desk, Pat, the receptionist, calls your name.

"What's the problem?" you ask.

"It's not my problem for much longer," Pat answers. She hands you a phone message. "She's your problem now."

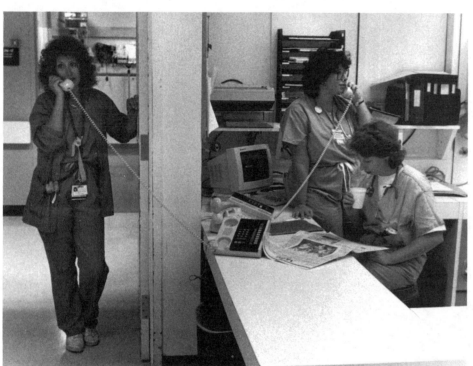

You read the message quickly. "It's not that Mrs. Jordan is a problem," you say. "She just *has* problems."

Problems is right. In her 82 years, Benita Jordan has outlived two of her four children and her husband. She's had pneumonia and rheumatoid arthritis. In the past 10 years, Mrs. Jordan has suffered sight loss, hearing loss, and weight gain. Through all this, she has kept her independence, living alone with no family nearby.

"She wants to come in tomorrow," says Pat.

You take the message to your phone.

"Mrs. Jordan? Hello, I'm calling from Dr. Peltier's office."

"Hi. I can't hear well. Speak up," says Mrs. Jordan.

You speak loudly. "How are you? I hear you want to come in."

"I'm not good. I have a cold and cough that won't go away. I'm feeling tired. My ankle is hurting, too, inside and out. I pretty much use the wheelchair whenever I leave the house now so I won't fall," Mrs. Jordan tells you.

"Well," you say, "we'd better see you tomorrow. What time can you come in?"

"The van can pick me up at 9:30 A.M.," she says.

"OK. We'll see you at 10:00 A.M. tomorrow. Bring your medication. Plan to stay about two hours," you tell her.

"Good. I'll remember. And I'll need to go to the accounting office, too," she states.

"No problem," you say. "See you tomorrow at 10:00."

Tomorrow's schedule is full. You must **adjust the schedule** to make time for Mrs. Jordan's visit. You'll also need to read Mrs. Jordan's medical record and **prioritize the information**. You will **plan your exam procedure** and **build a team** of people to help you. The volunteer guild can help Mrs. Jordan get to the lab, the pharmacy, and the accounting office after the exam. After that, you'll have to **use technology to update the medical record.**

SUMMARIZE THE TASKS

There are five tasks that you must accomplish in this lesson. These tasks are in **bold** type above. They are also listed below.

CATEGORY	TASK	ORDER	PAGE
Resources	*adjust the schedule*	____	8
Information	*prioritize medical information*	____	10
Systems	*plan an exam procedure*	____	13
Interpersonal	*build a team*	____	15
Technology and Tools	*update a medical record*	____	18

PLAN YOUR TIME.

As you think about the five tasks you must do in this lesson, you'll see that certain tasks may need to be done before others. Which task do you think should be done first?

Hint: Adjust _____. Write a *1* in the ORDER column above, next to this task.

What task should be done last? *Hint:* Update _____. Write a *5* in the ORDER column next to this task. Now decide an order for the other tasks. Write the numbers in the ORDER column.

The page order of the tasks in this lesson is not necessarily the order in which you would do them. Follow the order that you've decided above when you begin to work through the lesson.

THINK IT THROUGH

• What will you need to do these tasks? • What resources? • What information? • It's OK if you need more information at this point. You will find more information as you work through each task.

▶ Now go to the task *you* listed as 1 and continue the lesson.

Resources: Medical assistants make schedule changes each day. They evaluate the doctor's schedule, prioritize work, then develop an efficient patient schedule.

ADJUST THE SCHEDULE

Tomorrow's schedule is full for Dr. Peltier except for an opening at 11:30 A.M. Mrs. Jordan will need to be seen from 10:00 A.M. until at least 10:45 A.M. Here is Dr. Peltier's schedule:

TIME	NAME	AGE	REASON FOR VISIT
8:30	Pete Wilson	48	Mild chest pain two days ago
9:30	Helen Moore	37	Foot surgery check back/out of cast?
10:00	Sylvie Hernandez	25	Pregnant/7 month checkup
10:30	Jesse Withers	11	Regular checkup/needs measles vacc.
11:00	Luke Nguyen	2 mo.	Cold/cough for 2 days no temp.
11:30			
12:00 noon	Peltier on hospital rounds		

Dr. Peltier's clinic partner, Dr. Michaels, has appointment spaces open at 10:30 A.M. and in the afternoon. There are two clinic rules about adjusting schedules:

▶ Patients with immediate medical needs are seen first.
▶ All patients will be seen on their scheduled day.

For this task decide how to rearrange tomorrow's schedule to make room for Mrs. Jordan. Follow the clinic rules above and the blank doctor's schedule on page 145.

> ### VISUALIZE THE WHOLE TASK

Visualizing is "seeing a picture in your mind." Before you begin a task at work, you should picture it from beginning to end. Plan the steps you will take to complete the task. Ask yourself, • Do I need more information? • What problems could arise?

YOUR NOTES
How will you begin to rearrange the schedule? Write the steps you will take.
First, I will decide which patients do not have immediate medical needs. Then, I will _____
_____

Now you will begin to rearrange tomorrow's schedule.

Which patients on Dr. Peltier's schedule do not need to see the doctor right away? Can any patients scheduled between 10:00 A.M. and 10:45 A.M. be rescheduled? Find two other patients that could change. List them below.

PATIENTS TO CHANGE	MEDICAL NEEDS	NEW APPOINTMENT
Sylvie Hernandez	*regular checkup/ no emergency*	*could see Dr. Peltier at 11:30 or Dr. Michaels at 10:30 or in the afternoon*
1.		
2.		

Now use the blank schedule on page 145 to make a new schedule for tomorrow morning. The new schedule should reflect the changes made to accommodate Mrs. Jordan. Remember to follow the clinic rules and to include all the patients Dr. Peltier will see.

TASK RECAP

▶ Did you follow the clinic rules?
▶ Did you schedule Mrs. Jordan between 10:00 A.M. and 10:45 A.M.?
▶ Are all patients scheduled?

When you finish a task, it's a good idea to review your work. • How did your schedule changes work? • Were there any problems completing the task? • What would you do differently next time?

_____

_____

Information: Medical assistants spend time each day organizing information. This information can be verbal, such as patients' descriptions about how they feel. It can also be written, such as a doctor's notes, prescriptions, or test results from the lab.

*You should do the Resources task on page 8 before you begin this task.

PRIORITIZE MEDICAL INFORMATION

You've gotten Mrs. Jordan's chart from the medical records department. After skimming the chart, you need to evaluate it. You should review what Mrs. Jordan said on the phone. You should read any medical information you need to know, and then make recommendations to the doctor about Mrs. Jordan's exam.

For this task you will find medical information from these three sources: the phone conversation on page 6, the chart on page 19, and the medical information on page147. You will prioritize the information to decide what to tell the doctor.

VISUALIZE THE WHOLE TASK

Before you begin to prioritize the information, picture the task from beginning to end. • How will you decide what to tell the doctor? • What information do you need? • What should you do with that information?

YOUR NOTES
Finish the list below to help you organize your thoughts.

Information Needed	Purpose
Mrs. Jordan's medical chart	*to read about her medical history and her last doctor's appointment*

Now begin the task. Review the information from the chart (page 19) and the phone conversation (page 6). What medical problems has Mrs. Jordan had in the past? What medical problems is she currently having?

1. Past Problems: *pneumonia, rheumatoid arthritis,* _____

   _____

2. Present Problems: *cold, cough,* _____

   _____

Look at the medical information on page 147. Do any of Mrs. Jordan's current problems relate to her medical history? Could her cough be related to heart problems?

Hint: What is listed under "Heart Failure" that relates to Mrs. Jordan's current symptoms?

3. Classify the information from page 10 onto the chart below. List Mrs. Jordan's symptoms under the medical condition they may signify.

RHEUMATOID ARTHRITIS	PNEUMONIA	HEART FAILURE
_____	*cough*	*cough*
_____	_____	*rapid weight gain*
_____	_____	_____
_____	_____	_____
_____	_____	_____
_____	_____	_____
_____	_____	_____

4. Now finish the task. Look at the information you classified on the chart on page 11. Decide what information you will communicate to the doctor. Which symptoms or problems seem most important? What does the doctor need to know before Mrs. Jordan's visit?

List all information you feel is important on the Physician Communication form below. Be sure to include facts about her arthritis, pneumonia, and heart disease.

PHYSICIAN COMMUNICATION FORM

Instructions for use: Address communications. Sign communication, cross out when received and complete. Flip blue Alert clip to indicate message to be read.

Date/Time	To:

TASK RECAP

▶ Did you summarize the information for the doctor?
▶ Did you cover Mrs. Jordan's three areas of health problems?
▶ Is your handwriting readable?

REVIEW YOUR PLAN

When you finish a task, it's a good idea to review your work. • What steps did you take to prioritize medical information for the doctor? • How do you think your information will help focus the doctor's exam?

_____

_____

Systems: Every medical facility has procedures for staff to follow. Medical assistants must understand these systems, especially the systems that affect patient flow. The medical assistant's job is to follow **procedures** and move patients through their visits quickly and effectively.

You should do the Resources task on page 8 before you begin this task.

PLAN AN EXAM PROCEDURE

You must plan your part of Mrs. Jordan's medical exam. Mrs. Jordan will need special help during the exam. She's in a wheelchair, for one, and she has had sight and hearing loss.

For this task you will plan an exam procedure that accommodates Mrs. Jordan's special needs.

VISUALIZE THE WHOLE TASK

Before you begin the exam procedure, picture the task from beginning to end. • What can you do to help Mrs. Jordan through the exam? • What will she need help with?

YOUR NOTES
How will Mrs. Jordan's needs change the usual exam procedure? List your ideas below.   *Since Mrs. Jordan is in a wheelchair,* _____   _____   _____

COMPLETE THE TASK

1. Skim through the Exam Procedure list on page 14. Put an *X* next to each step you think Mrs. Jordan will need help with.

2. For each step you marked with an *X*, think about what you can do to help Mrs. Jordan. List your adjustment on the line beneath each step.

Medical Assistant Exam Procedure

Before physician's exam:

1. set up exam room

   leave extra room for the wheelchair

2. call patient to exam room

   _____

3. make patient comfortable on exam table

   _____

4. take patient's vital signs:

   a. temperature

   b. blood pressure

   c. height and weight

   d. pulse and respiration

5. ask about new symptoms

   _____

   _____

6. record information

   _____

7. tell doctor when patient is ready

   _____

After physician's exam:

8. schedule tests

   _____

9. complete lab/pharmacy requests

   _____

10. direct patient to next step

    _____

11. prepare exam room for next patient

    _____

12. record patient information in chart

    _____

TASK RECAP

▶ Did you think through the whole exam and consider what might be difficult for Mrs. Jordan?

▶ Did you create ways to help her but still perform the exam?

REVIEW YOUR PLAN

When you finish a task, it's a good idea to review your work. Review the steps you took to adjust the exam procedure. • Are you ready for Mrs. Jordan? • Will the exam go smoothly with your adjustments? • Do you foresee any problems?

_____

_____

Interpersonal: Medical assistants must work well with people. They must interact with patients, office staff, nurses, doctors, and medical technicians. Medical assistants must act as cooperative and flexible members of a team.

You should do the Resources task on page 8 before you begin this task.

BUILD A TEAM

You will be responsible for Mrs. Jordan's visit since she can't be as independent as most patients. Now you must plan how a team of people can help Mrs. Jordan. All of the services she needs today are in the same clinic building. Mrs. Jordan will need help

- ▶ getting in and out of her wheelchair
- ▶ getting through the exam
- ▶ getting medications from the pharmacy
- ▶ completing any lab tests the doctor orders

For this task you will build a team of people to help Mrs. Jordan throughout her whole clinic visit. You will think about how to build a team. Then you'll work with a partner to practice building one. Your partner can be a classmate, a teacher, a family member, or a friend.

VISUALIZE THE WHOLE TASK

Before you begin to build a team, picture the task from beginning to end. • What does Mrs. Jordan need help with? • Who can you call for help? • Look at the list above and reread the the top of page 14 for ideas.

YOUR NOTES
List some of your ideas about building a team below.
For help getting Mrs. Jordan in and out of her wheelchair, I could request a volunteer from
the volunteer's guild. For help getting her through the exam, I could

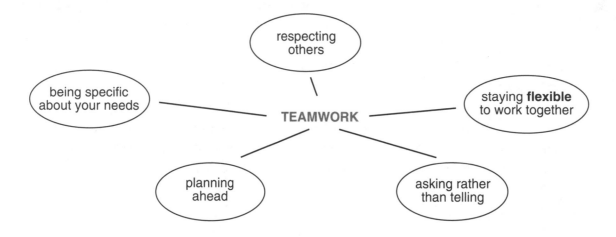

Think about the diagram above. How can you be **flexible** with your team members when asking for help for Mrs. Jordan?

by compromising—meeting the person halfway

Question: *"If you're not available at 10:00, would you be free at 10:30?"*

1. How can you **show respect** when asking for help?

   _____

   Question: _____

   _____

2. How can you **plan ahead** when building a team?

   _____

   Question: _____

   _____

3. How can you **be specific** when asking for help?

   _____

   Question: _____

   _____

4. How can you **ask, not demand**?

_____

Question: _____

_____

5. Now it's time to build the team. Ask your partner to play one of the five possible team members below. Using the ideas you wrote on page 16, ask this person for help with Mrs. Jordan's needs.

Possible team members:

▶ pharmacy assistant
▶ clinic volunteer
▶ accounting clerk
▶ lab technician
▶ medical receptionist

Be sure to cover all five areas of teamwork:

▶ respecting others
▶ being specific
▶ planning ahead
▶ asking rather than telling
▶ staying flexible

TASK RECAP

▶ Did you ask for help with something Mrs. Jordan will need?
▶ Did you follow the five areas of teamwork?
▶ Did your partner agree to work with your team?

REVIEW YOUR PLAN

When you finish a task, it's a good idea to review your work. • How did your questions help build a team? • How would you improve your questions next time?

_____

_____

_____

Technology and Tools: Medical assistants use technology every day. They use computers to maintain and update medical records. They choose the proper machines to help diagnose patients. They also set up and operate machines such as an EKG (electrocardiograph), which records electric currents produced by the heart.

You should do the Resources task on page 8 before you begin this task.

UPDATE A MEDICAL RECORD

Mrs. Jordan is now being examined by Dr. Peltier. It was good that she phoned when she did. She'd gained 10 pounds since her last visit, even though she had not overeaten. Her eyes were watery and she coughed every two to three minutes. She had great difficulty moving from the wheelchair to the exam table—partly because her ankle was so swollen.

Here are Mrs. Jordan's current vital signs:

temperature (T)	weight	blood pressure (BP)	pulse	respiration
102.4	208	160 over 95	85	20 with wheezing

For this task you will update Mrs. Jordan's medical record with information from her visit today. You will decide what information to add to the record. Then you will use a word processor or a typewriter to update her record on the Physician Progress Record on page 145.

VISUALIZE THE WHOLE TASK

Before you begin to update the record, picture the task from beginning to end.
• Where will you get the information to update the record?

YOUR NOTES

You have information from Mrs. Jordan's phone call (page 6) and from the exam results. What information could you include on the medical record?

I could include information she gave me over the phone such as a cold and cough that

won't go away. I could _____

_____

_____

Now begin to complete the task. Below is Mrs. Jordan's chart *before* her appointment.

▶ What information does it include?

▶ How is the information recorded (in short phrases, or in a list)?

<table>
<tr>
<td colspan="3">GROUP HEALTH HOSPITAL
PHYSICIAN PROGRESS RECORD</td>
</tr>
<tr>
<td>DATE OF ADMISSION</td>
<td>TIME</td>
<td>JORDAN, BENITA S. #7749092</td>
</tr>
<tr>
<td>DATE &
TIME</td>
<td colspan="2">NOTE PROGRESS OF PATIENT, COMPLICATIONS, CONSULTATION, CHANGE IN
DIAGNOSIS, CONDITION ON DISCHARGE AND INSTRUCTIONS TO PATIENT</td>
</tr>
<tr>
<td>9/22/93</td>
<td colspan="2">Phoned 9/21 complaining of fatigue, some abdominal pain, and cough.</td>
</tr>
<tr>
<td>9/22 A.M.</td>
<td colspan="2">Visited office. Cough produces yellow sputum
5-10 minute spans; painful breathing</td>
</tr>
<tr>
<td></td>
<td colspan="2">Vitals: T: 101.4 BP: 150/95 Respiration: 18 no wheezing
Pulse: 80; not erratic   Weight: 198</td>
</tr>
<tr>
<td></td>
<td colspan="2">Peltier renewed Digitalis: prescribed Guaifenesin for cough
Patient should monitor weight, revisit if cough persists</td>
</tr>
<tr>
<td></td>
<td colspan="2"></td>
</tr>
</table>

1. Decide what information you will add to Mrs. Jordan's record. List it below.

<table>
<tr>
<td></td>
<td>*Phoned complaining of*</td>
</tr>
<tr>
<td></td>
<td></td>
</tr>
<tr>
<td></td>
<td></td>
</tr>
</table>

2. Now use a word processor or a typewriter to update Mrs. Jordan's record on the blank Physician Progress Record on page 145. When adding to the medical record, use short phrases as used on the chart above.

TASK RECAP

▶ Did you update the record on page 145?

▶ Did you include all information that could be important?

When you finish a task, it's a good idea to review your work. • What steps did you follow to update the medical record? • What would you do differently next time?

USE WHAT YOU'VE LEARNED

You have been learning a variety of skills within the context of being a medical assistant. Some of the skills are:

▶ adjusting a schedule
▶ prioritizing information
▶ changing a procedure to meet the needs of a client
▶ requesting help and building a team
▶ using technology to record information

1. Name two other jobs that might require these skills. How might these skills be put to use?

   Example: *a teacher requests help from another teacher when working together with a class*

   _____

   _____

2. Is there anywhere else you've used these skills? Where?

   Example: *at home I adjust the schedule when my wife has to work late*

   _____

   _____

3. Which of these skills were the most difficult for you? Why?

   _____

   _____

   _____

4. How could you practice these difficult skills?

   _____

   _____

   _____

   _____

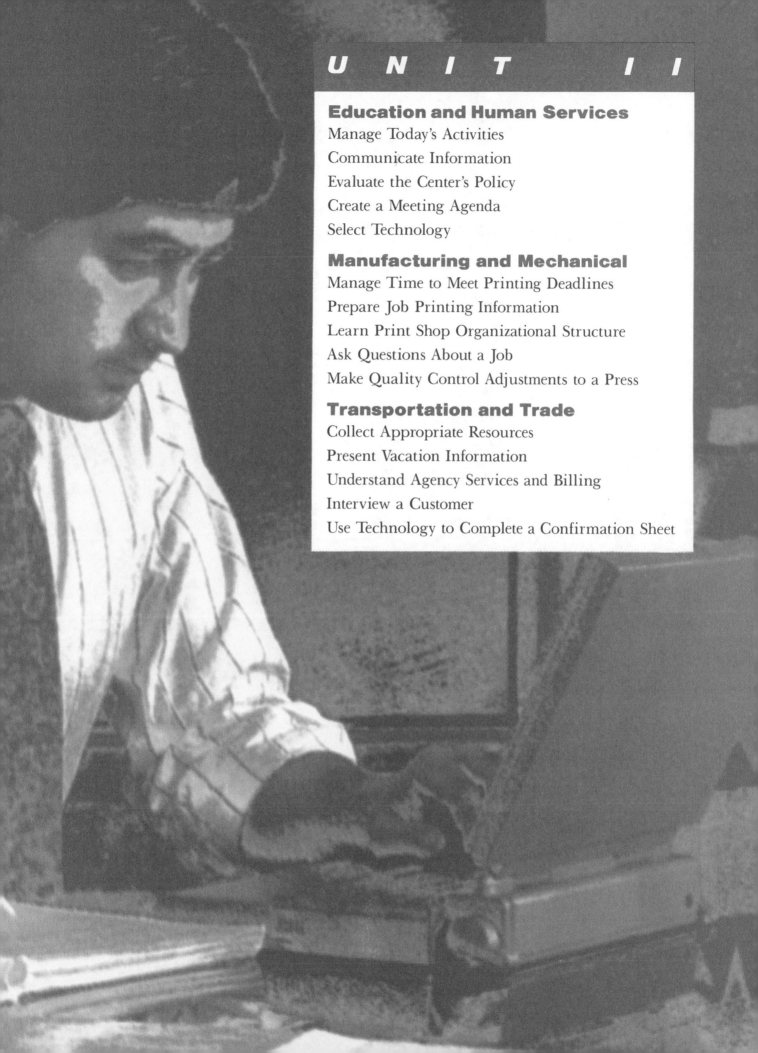

UNIT II

Education and Human Services

Manage Today's Activities

Communicate Information

Evaluate the Center's Policy

Create a Meeting Agenda

Select Technology

Manufacturing and Mechanical

Manage Time to Meet Printing Deadlines

Prepare Job Printing Information

Learn Print Shop Organizational Structure

Ask Questions About a Job

Make Quality Control Adjustments to a Press

Transportation and Trade

Collect Appropriate Resources

Present Vacation Information

Understand Agency Services and Billing

Interview a Customer

Use Technology to Complete a Confirmation Sheet

■■■EDUCATION & HUMAN SERVICES

Compared to all jobs, the growth rate for education and human services jobs is expected to be much higher over the next 10 years. The rising U.S. population, rising school enrollments, and a growing number of elderly citizens lead to this job growth. Workers in this field deal with the physical and emotional needs of others. The work requires patience, the ability to motivate others, and some leadership and **administrative** abilities.

SOME SKILLS YOU WILL PRACTICE IN THIS LESSON

- ▶ Manage Activities
- ▶ Communicate Information
- ▶ Evaluate a Policy
- ▶ Create a Meeting Agenda
- ▶ Select Technology

Childcare workers work within the education and human services career cluster. Childcare workers are responsible for the overall health, nutrition, and social welfare of children in their care. They are employed in large childcare centers and in smaller daycare centers. In larger facilities, childcare workers may be responsible only for children. Smaller childcare facilities may ask childcare workers to handle administrative tasks as well.

Childcare workers must be team members. They must follow their facility's rules, manage time, and deal with all kinds of information while meeting the needs of the children left in their care.

SOME RELATED JOBS

preschool teacher
teacher's assistant
recreation leader
tutor

A Little Class

It's parent conference time at the College Place Childcare Center. Marilyn Schwartz, the center director, dreads what these important conferences do to the center's schedule. It's hard to schedule meetings with the children's parents, who all take classes at the college.

As a childcare worker at College Place, you have new responsibilities because of the parent conferences. While Marilyn and the instructors are in conferences, you must take over caring for the children. Right now, for example, it's your responsibility to schedule children's activities to cover three days of conferences.

As you watch the children arrive at school, you realize how varied your activities will need to be. The children all have different interests and learning styles.

"Good morning, Tina," you say to the last child to arrive. Tina doesn't answer.

You hear Tishan calling. "We're astronauts flying to the moon. Would you stand here and be the moon?"

"Maybe Tina would like to be the moon," you say, as you see Tina watching the children.

"Tina never plays with us. She doesn't like our games," says Nick. He adds, "I don't even think she knows what the moon is."

You see Tina quietly close the bathroom door behind her.

During outside play, you see Tina trying to fix a broken bike pedal.

"Tina, you've put the pieces back exactly right," you say. Tina smiles. "Good job. We'll need a screwdriver to tighten it, though. Have you ever used a screwdriver?"

Before Tina can answer, Nick runs past, skidding too close for fun. The next time Nick skids by, Tina puts her foot out. Nick falls, scraping his arm and face. He starts to cry.

What will you do? You don't want to interrupt Marilyn's parent conference. You'd like to take the lead in finding a solution to the problem.

What will you do? You won't need to solve this problem alone. But you will have to **manage the activities** so that you'll have extra time to deal with it. You will need to **communicate information** about what happened on the playground and **evaluate the Center's policy** for these situations. You will **create a meeting agenda** to work the problem out. Finally, you will **select technology** at the Center that could help Tina and Nick get along.

SUMMARIZE THE TASKS

There are five tasks that you must accomplish in this lesson. These tasks are in **bold** type above. Below, write each task next to the correct category. Two have been completed for you.

CATEGORY	TASK	ORDER	PAGE
Resources	*manage today's activities*	____	26
Information	*communicate information*	____	28
Systems	_____	____	30
Interpersonal	_____	____	32
Technology and Tools	_____	____	34

PLAN YOUR TIME

Of the five tasks, which do you think should be done right away? In the ORDER column above, number the tasks in the order you will complete them.

The page order of the tasks in this workbook is not necessarily the order in which you would do them. Follow the order that you've decided above when you begin to work through the lesson.

THINK IT THROUGH

• What will you need to do these tasks? • What resources? • What people? • What information? It's OK if you need more information at this point. You will find more information as you work through each task.

▶ Now go to the task *you* listed as 1 and continue the lesson.

Resources: Childcare workers must manage their time to create a positive environment for children. They have many routine tasks, such as cleaning, completing paperwork, feeding children, and planning activities. They must also be flexible enough to respond to children's other needs.

MANAGE TODAY'S ACTIVITIES

It is only 10:00 A.M. and you have your hands full. You need to schedule today's activities. You also need to clean Nick's scrapes and plan what to do about the trouble between Tina and Nick. Luckily, David, another childcare worker, has just arrived and will be able to help.

You'll need to schedule the following regular activities:

two snacks (½ hour each)   freeplay (1 hour)

lunch and cleanup (1 hour)   outdoor play (1 hour)

arts and crafts (1 hour)   indoor gym (½ hour)

music (½ hour)   storytime (½ hour)

naptime (1 hour)   final cleanup (½ hour)

Naptime is usually from 1:30 to 2:30 P.M. Lunch and cleanup are usually scheduled from 12:00 to 1:00.

For this task you will fill out a schedule of today's activities. You will decide who will monitor the activities and plan time to take care of the problem between Tina and Nick.

VISUALIZE THE WHOLE TASK

Before you plan the day's activities, picture the task from beginning to end. • Are certain times of day better for certain activities? • How can you build time to deal with Nick and Tina?

YOUR NOTES
How will you decide when to schedule different activities? Write your ideas below.

TIME	ACTIVITY	ASSIGNED STAFFPERSON: you/David
10:00–10:30		
10:30–11:00		
11:00–12:00		
12:00–1:00	*lunch and cleanup*	
1:00–1:30		
1:30–2:30	*naptime*	
2:30–3:00		
3:00–4:00		
4:00–4:30		
4:30–5:30		
5:30–6:00		

COMPLETE THE TASK

Fill out the schedule above with the daily activities listed on page 26. Next, decide which staffperson will monitor each activity, you or David. Finally, build time into the schedule for you to handle Nick's scrapes and the problem between Nick and Tina. *Hint:* You may want to deal with the two children during a time when David can supervise the other children.

TASK RECAP

▶ Is each daily activity covered?
▶ Is at least one staffperson watching the children at all times?
▶ Are the activities scheduled at appropriate times?

REVIEW YOUR PLAN

If you had to plan this schedule over again, would you do anything differently? • What? • Why? List your ideas below.

_____

_____

Information: Childcare workers must be good listeners and speakers. Much of the information shared throughout a day is verbal, but there is also written record keeping. Childcare workers must communicate with children, parents, and other staff.

COMMUNICATE INFORMATION

So far, only you, Nick, and Tina know about the playground incident. You must decide how to deal with the situation. You want both of them to take responsibility for their actions; you also want them to stop fighting. You'll need to tell their parents and the rest of the staff about the incident. You'd like everyone to work together to create a positive outcome to this problem.

For this task you will decide how to tell everyone involved about the playground incident. You will outline a conversation with one of the people you must talk with.

VISUALIZE THE WHOLE TASK

Before you begin to talk with others, picture the task from beginning to end. • Exactly what happened between Nick and Tina? Reread the story on page 24. • What is your goal? • How can you create a positive outcome from this situation?

YOUR NOTES
How will you create a positive outcome from this situation? Write your ideas below.
_____
_____

COMPLETE THE TASK

Begin the task by writing a few ideas of what you'll say to each person. Use the chart as a sample. Write your ideas on another sheet of paper.

Marilyn	David	Nick	Tina	Nick's parents	Tina's parents
This morning, Nick teased Tina and made her feel bad. During outside play, Nick…					

Now you will practice one of the conversations by outlining it below. Which person would you like to talk with?

Marilyn   David   Nick   Tina   Nick's parents   Tina's parents

With that person in mind, create a conversation outline below. Use your ideas from the chart on page 28. Keep in mind the following points:

▶ How will you introduce the problem?
▶ What questions might you have to answer?
▶ How can you keep the situation positive?

1. Introduction: *Who are you? What do you need to talk about?*

2. Retell Incident: *What happened?*

3. Answer Questions/Concerns: *What questions might you have to answer?*

4. Request Ideas to Resolve Problem: *What ideas might this person have?*

TASK RECAP

▶ Did you fill in all parts of the outline?
▶ Did you work toward a positive outcome?

REVIEW YOUR PLAN

Review the information you've written above. • Are you sure the information is presented clearly? • How will the conversation you've planned help you solve the problem?

_____

_____

Systems: Childcare workers must work within several systems. Licensed facilities are regulated by the government. They have rules for student-teacher ratios, safety, and other quality standards. Each childcare facility also has its own set of **policies**. Childcare workers must understand these policies and suggest changes as needed.

EVALUATE THE CENTER'S POLICY

Holding both Nick's and Tina's hands, you come in from outside play. They know that after Nick's scrapes are attended to, they'll have separate time-outs. You know that five-minute time-outs won't solve this problem.

The Center's policy states:

▶ Any child physically injuring another must be disciplined.
▶ Parents must be informed of incidents.
▶ Staff will discuss any problems in weekly meetings.
▶ A family may face withdrawal from the Center if its child's behavior doesn't improve.

For this task you will decide how to implement the Center's policy for the situation between Nick and Tina. You will recommend how to change part of the policy so that it's more fair at times when two children are at fault.

Before you begin to evaluate the policy, picture the task from beginning to end.
• According to the policy, who should be disciplined? • Who should be told about the problem? • What steps should you take to follow the policy?

YOUR NOTES
Decide what steps you'll take to follow and evaluate the policy. What will you do first? Second? Write your ideas below.
First, I will read the policy again. Then, I will _____
_____

1. Evaluate how the Center's policy applies to this situation. Of the two children, which one physically injured the other?

   _____

2. According to the Center's policy, Tina should be disciplined. Is Tina the only one at fault, or should both children share responsibility?

   _____

3. If you believe that both children should share the responsibility, you must reconsider the Center's policy. In what ways could the policy be changed to reflect both children's involvement in hurting each other?

   _____

   _____

4. With whom should you discuss these policy changes? _____

   _____

5. Who do you think has final approval of policy changes? _____

6. Marilyn, the Center's director, agrees with you that the policy should be changed to include problems like Tina and Nick had. In the space below, rewrite the line from the Center's policy to reflect your recommended change.

   * Any child physically injuring another must be disciplined.

   _____

   _____

TASK RECAP

▶ Does your new policy apply to incidents in which children are cruel but don't physically hurt others?

Now that you've worked with the Center's policy, how do you feel about it? • How will your new policy improve the Center in the future? • What did you learn about policies in general?

_____

_____

Interpersonal: Childcare workers spend all of their working hours with people. They need to cooperate with others, share tasks, and encourage children and other staff members. Working as a team member helps everyone. It provides a positive model for children and for parents.

CREATE A MEETING AGENDA

All the adults involved want to meet to try to resolve the children's problems. The problem is that there are several opinions about just what should happen.

- ▶ Nick's mother wants Tina out of the Center.
- ▶ Tina's father doesn't want that to happen. He promises to discipline Tina.
- ▶ You and Marilyn agree that Tina should stay in school, but everyone should try to change both Tina's and Nick's behavior.

Since Marilyn has parent conferences scheduled, she won't be present at the meeting. The children's parents have come to the Center to meet with you. David is handling the rest of the children for the last hour of the day.

Here is a list Marilyn gives you of common meeting elements:

time limit	reason for meeting	review
decision making	agenda	varied viewpoints
summary	closing	goals
consensus	introductions	assignments made

For this task you will plan to run the meeting with the children's parents. You will create an agenda for the meeting that covers all of the elements listed above. Finally, you will share ideas with a classmate and compare your agendas.

VISUALIZE THE WHOLE TASK

Before you prepare the meeting agenda, picture the task from beginning to end. • Do you understand the meaning of each meeting element listed above? • How can you prepare for the different opinions people will have?

YOUR NOTES

The list of meeting elements above is not in order. Decide in what order you'd like to address each element. List them in order below.

introductions, reason for meeting, _____

_____

MEETING AGENDA	what to cover	who is responsible
1.		
2.		
3.		
4.		
5.		
6.		
7.		
8.		
9.		
10.		
11.		
12.		

COMPLETE THE TASK

Copy your agenda order from your notes on page 32 onto the schedule above.
Consider the purpose behind each agenda item. On the schedule, make notes about
what should be covered in each step. Next, decide who is responsible for each element.
(*Hint:* For example, each person can be responsible for introducing himself or
herself.)

Now compare your agenda with a classmate's. Would both agendas work in a meeting?
Why or why not?

TASK RECAP

▶ Did you fill out each line on the agenda?
▶ Did you share responsibility so that you aren't in charge of everything?

REVIEW YOUR PLAN

Now that you've created a meeting agenda, how do you think it will work? • How would
you change the agenda next time?

Technology and Tools: New technology designed to help children learn appears on the market constantly. Childcare workers must know about new learning technologies. This awareness lets them choose better ways to help children learn and grow.

SELECT TECHNOLOGY FOR TINA

You would like Tina to be happy at the Center and to make some friends. You know that she'll be happier if you build on her strengths. You've noticed that she likes to do certain things more than others.

This morning on the playground, Tina fixed her tricycle pedal. She enjoys building. She is coordinated and capable when it comes to putting things together. Often she brings hand-held electronic games to school. The other children are curious but too timid to ask Tina about her games. The activities she enjoys most are ones in which she can use her hands and see a final product.

The following tools and technology are available at the Center:

carpentry center	microphone	tape recorder
board games	calculator	typewriter
magnifying glass	computer	stencils
building blocks	tricycle	electronic keyboard

For this task you will choose three tools or technologies for Tina to play with. You'll choose toys that match her strengths and also might help her make friends with other children in her class.

VISUALIZE THE WHOLE TASK

Before you choose toys for Tina, picture the task from beginning to end. • What is Tina good at? • What might be a good way to encourage Tina to make friends?

YOUR NOTES
How will you decide which toys to choose? What steps will you take?
First, I will think about what Tina is good at. Then, I will _____
_____
_____

Choose three tools or technologies from the list on page 34 that you think will match Tina's skills and interests. List them below. Next to each toy, list the skills it involves. Explain why you think it would be a good match for Tina.

Toy/Technology	Skill	Why a good match?
tape recorder	electronic skill, speaking and listening skills	Tina might enjoy using her electronic skills and creating a tape to share with others
1.		
2.		
3.		

4. Now choose one toy or technology from the chart above. If Tina is successful with this tool, how could this success help her make friends in her class? List some ideas below.

_____

_____

TASK RECAP

► Did you choose tools that Tina will probably enjoy?
► Did you list ways to help Tina make friends?

Now that you've chosen toys for Tina, what will you do if she rejects one of them?
• How will you respond? • What suggestions will you make? List your ideas.

_____

_____

_____

USE WHAT YOU'VE LEARNED

You've been learning a variety of skills within the context of being a childcare worker. Some of these skills are

- ► managing time to complete extra tasks
- ► changing a procedure
- ► communicating a problem
- ► planning a meeting
- ► learning or teaching a new technology

1. Name two other jobs that might require these skills. How might these skills be put to use?

   Example: *a swim instructor may change a procedure to let a frightened child use a life jacket*

   _____

   _____

2. Is there anywhere else you've used these skills? Where?

   Example: *I communicate a problem when I explain to a teacher why I don't understand*

   *something*_____

   _____

3. Now that you've completed the tasks in this lesson, can you think of two new tasks at work or at home that you might try? What are they?

   _____

   _____

   _____

   _____

■■■ MANUFACTURING/MECHANICAL

The growth rate for manufacturing and mechanical jobs is expected to be about the same as that for all jobs over the next decade. In manufacturing firms, the technical, professional, and managerial jobs will increase. Workers in manufacturing deal with machines or hand tools to make products. Some workers help design and build the machines. Others operate or maintain the machines to create products.

SOME SKILLS YOU WILL PRACTICE IN THIS LESSON

- ▶ Manage Time to Meet Deadlines
- ▶ Prepare Information
- ▶ Learn an Organizational Structure
- ▶ Ask Questions About a Job
- ▶ Make Quality Control Adjustments

One job within the manufacturing and mechanical career cluster is offset press operator. These operators run presses that print all kinds of information you use every day: forms, brochures, books, manuals, stationery, and business cards. To do this, offset press operators control the large presses that press paper against an inked metal plate to print information.

Offset press operators begin by gathering materials to print a document: ink, paper, and the metal plate. They set the machine up to operate, load the paper, and begin the press. While the document is being printed, offset press operators monitor the quality of the printing and adjust the press as required.

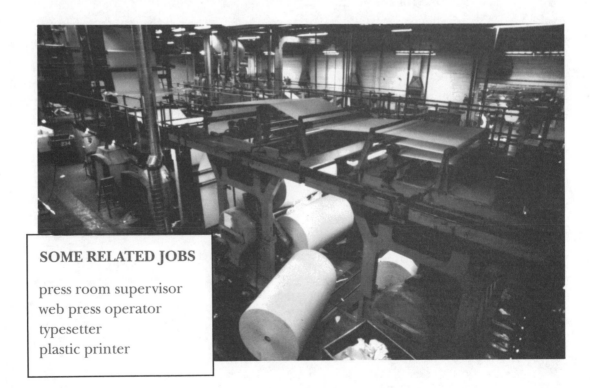

SOME RELATED JOBS

press room supervisor
web press operator
typesetter
plastic printer

A Pressing Day

The minute you get out of your car in the Fine Printing parking lot this morning, other employees ask how you're doing.

"Came back again today?" Henry, the other press operator, remarks. "I thought you'd give up on us after all the overtime you put in last week."

Last week, your second week on the job, had been hard. You hope last week was not a typical week here at Fine Printing. After all, you're still getting to know the shop and employees.

"Don't tell me we're heading into another week like that," you reply.

Laughing, Henry says, "I haven't even checked the schedule with Leon yet. Let's go see what he has in store for us."

Leon is the shop manager. He takes orders, schedules all the work, supervises the employees, and knows the shop like the back of his hand.

Leon hands Henry a stack of yellow job orders. Henry looks surprised. Leon quickly says, "Hey, don't look so worried. It isn't a repeat of last week. That stack is for both of you today. I thought you two could divide these orders up to make your schedules. It looks like we have some time to think today."

As Henry looks through the job orders, you wonder if today you'll have time to learn more about the shop: who does what, how long they've been in the printing business, how an order moves from beginning to end.

"OK, you can stop snooping now and get to work," Henry teases, noticing you look closely at the typesetter's computer. "How about doing a rerun today? One of our biggest customers has requested more letterhead."

"Sure, let's get those machines warmed up," you reply.

As you begin the day, you think through what you know of the tasks ahead of you. You and Henry need to make your schedules and **manage time to meet deadlines**. You'll have to **prepare information** for the rerun order. Today may be a good day for you to **learn the shop's organizational structure** and to **ask questions about your co-workers' jobs**. For the rerun order, you know you'll need to check the plates, prepare the ink and paper, and **make adjustments to the press as necessary**.

SUMMARIZE THE TASKS

There are five tasks that you must accomplish in this lesson. These tasks are in **bold** type above. Below, write each task next to the correct category.

CATEGORY	TASK	ORDER	PAGE
Resources	_____	____	40
Information	_____	____	42
Systems	*learn the shop's organizational structure*	*1*	44
Interpersonal	_____	____	46
Technology and Tools	_____	____	48

PLAN YOUR TIME

Of the five tasks, are there some that should be done before others? *Hint:* Would you need to prepare information for the rerun order before you make adjustments to the press? In the ORDER column above, number the tasks in the order you will complete them.

The page order of the tasks in this workbook is not necessarily the order in which you would do them. Follow the order that you've decided above when you begin to work through the lesson.

THINK IT THROUGH

• What will you need to do the tasks? • What resources? • What people? • What other information do you need? It's OK if you need more information at this point. You will find more information as you work through each task.

▶ Now go to the task listed as 1 and continue the lesson.

Resources: Offset press operators are under pressure to perform each printing job quickly and to produce a high-quality product. If there is a problem with the deadlines on a job, the operator must try to solve the problem. He or she must work with other staff as necessary.

* You should do the Systems task on page 44 before beginning this task.

MANAGE TIME TO MEET PRINTING DEADLINES

You've noticed a problem with Homeland's job order. Homeland ordered 3,000 more copies of their letterhead, but requested a slight change. The company president, Carl Mikolic, passed away recently and left his daughter Carol in charge of the company. Homeland requested that the new letterhead read *Carol* instead of *Carl* above the title of President.

Any change to an existing plate requires a new plate to be created so you need to make a new plate.

It's clear now that you won't be able to print the Homeland order first today. It will take at least an hour for you to fit this into your schedule, then another 20 minutes to produce a new plate. You have to look at your schedule and make new plans.

It is now 8:15 A.M. Because the Homeland order is postponed for now, you are free until 10:00 A.M., when the new Homeland plate will be ready. Either you or Henry will have to fit the Homeland order in sometime today.

For this task you'll rearrange the printing schedule to adjust for the change on the Homeland order.

VISUALIZE THE WHOLE TASK

Before you revise your schedule, picture the task from beginning to end. • What will you do first? • What steps will you take to change the schedule?

YOUR NOTES
How will you make changes to your schedule? • Who will you work with on the schedule changes? • Who will you check with when you've created a new schedule? List your ideas below.
_____
_____
_____

Henry's schedule		Your schedule	
8:00 A.M.	RR + 2,000	8:00 A.M.	~~RR + 3,000~~ cancelled
9:00 A.M.		9:00 A.M.	
10:00 A.M.	RR + 3,000	10:00 A.M.	
11:00 A.M.		11:00 A.M.	RR + 1,000
12:00 P.M.	Lunch	12:00 P.M.	
1:00 P.M.	RR + 2,000	1:00 P.M.	Lunch
2:00 P.M.		2:00 P.M.	NP + 6,000
3:00 P.M.	3:30 NP + 1,500	3:00 P.M.	
4:00 P.M.		4:00 P.M.	
5:00 P.M.		5:00 P.M.	

RR—rerun

NP—new plate

Number of copies follows the + sign.

Each job takes about 45 minutes to prepare.

Each run of 3,000 copies takes about an hour to produce.

COMPLETE THE TASK

Study the schedule and the explanation above. Rearrange it so that you or Henry can do the Homeland order today. You can switch the times for jobs already scheduled. You can also switch jobs with Henry if necessary. *Hint:* Be sure to allow time for both preparation and printing.

TASK RECAP

▶ Check your revised schedule. Did you give yourself enough time to prepare and print each job?

▶ Does your revised schedule allow you to leave at 5:00 P.M.?

REVIEW YOUR PLAN

Now that you've revised your schedule to allow for the Homeland change, how did it go? • Is there anything you'd do differently when changing a schedule next time?

Information: Before an offset press operator can print a job, he or she must interpret the job order. From the order, the operator can see exactly what the job requires.

* You should do the Systems task on page 44 before beginning this task.

PREPARE JOB PRINTING INFORMATION

The Homeland order is the first one of the day. Homeland, a real estate company, is requesting more letterhead. You need to

- ▶ study the job order
- ▶ get the plate from the company file
- ▶ check the condition of the plate before you prepare the press

The job order will specify what the customer wants, including the type of paper, ink color, binding requirements, number of copies, and a deadline for the job.

For this job you will collect and prepare job printing information. You will need to study the job order on page 149.

You know that the job order will give you much of the information you need. Before you dive into the task, read the narrative on page 38. Below, list the information that you now know and the information that you still need to know in order to do this job.

I know	Need to know
job is a letterhead rerun	*which press will I use?*

VISUALIZE THE WHOLE TASK

Before you begin to prepare the information, picture the task from beginning to end.
• How will you do this job? • Who will you need to talk with? • Is there anything in your "need to know" column that you can't find on the order form?

YOUR NOTES
How will you collect and interpret the information you need to print the Homeland Realty rerun? List the steps you will follow.
First, I will read the job order and request the plates from

Look at the job order on page 149. Answer the following questions about the Homeland rerun.

1. What paper stock will you use?_____

2. What ink has been requested? _____

3. Who took the order?_____

4. Is there any binding requested? _____

5. What press will be running this order?_____

6. What instructions did the customer give? _____

7. Do you anticipate any problems with these instructions? _____

8. If so, what problems? _____

9. Who should you talk with at Homeland about any problems? _____

TASK RECAP

▶ Did you answer all the questions above?
▶ Do you understand the meaning of each term used?

REVIEW YOUR PLAN

Now that you have reviewed the job order, think about it. • How did you read the job order? • What was easy? • What was hard?

_____

_____

_____

Systems: Offset press operators must understand how the print shop is organized and operated. They must learn the shop's organizational system as well as job order procedures. They also need to learn where to go for information.

LEARN PRINT SHOP ORGANIZATIONAL STRUCTURE

Congratulations on scheduling time to learn more about the print shop. Leon, the shop manager, has given you two diagrams: one detailing the print shop organization, and one about the offset lithographic press.

For this task you will study the diagrams on pages 151 and 153. You will learn more about the print shop and about your job as an offset press operator. Finally, you will number the order in which processes occur in the print shop and on the press.

VISUALIZE THE WHOLE TASK

Before you begin to learn about the print shop, picture the task from beginning to end. Look at the diagram on page 151. You are the press operator, but other employees are important to your work. • Who takes the job order? • Who will you ask for more information on a job order? • What parts of an order are not part of your job?

YOUR NOTES
What happens to an order before you see it? Who else works on it? List the people below.
the shop manager (takes the customer's order and prepares a cost estimate)
typesetter and pasteup (

Review the diagrams on pages 151 and 153. Be sure you can find each process on the list below.

After you've reviewed the diagrams, decide whether each process is part of the offset press operator's duties. If it is, put an *X* on the line next to it. Finally, number the processes from 1 to 18, following the order in which a job proceeds through the print shop, through your press, and to delivery to the customer.

Offset Press Operator Duty?	Process	Order in Process
____	billing the customer	____
____	inking rollers	____
____	shipping	____
____	adjusting the ink rollers	____
____	setting the type	____
____	developing film	____
____	checking a sample against the proof	____
____	estimating document cost	____
____	making the plate	____
____	attaching plate to cylinder	____
____	binding	____
____	writing a packing list	____
____	checking the water level	____
____	taking the customer order	____
____	completing job order form	____
____	packing the printed documents	____
____	checking the paper stock	____
____	printing documents	____

TASK RECAP

▶ Did you decide which tasks were offset press operator's duties?
▶ Did you number the tasks from 1–18 in a logical order?

Think about the steps you followed to learn the print shop and press systems. • What was difficult? • What was easy?

_____

_____

Interpersonal: No matter how big or small the shop, offset press operators need to work well with others. In a small shop, operators may have more contact with customers. Bigger shops isolate the press operators from customers but have employee teams communicating with each other to produce a quality product.

* You should do the Systems task on page 44 before beginning this task.

ASK QUESTIONS ABOUT A JOB

"Have you two operators gotten your schedules worked out for the day?" Leon asks.

"We just finished," Henry replies. "Looks like a busy one."

Leon turns to you. He says, "Sometime soon I'd like you to build in time to see the other parts of the shop, and get to know all of us."

You answer, "I'd like that too. I have a lot to learn from everyone here. I'll see if there's any room today, and let you know."

Henry was right. It's so busy that the only time you have free today is at lunch. You decide to make the most of it. You decide it might be smart to talk with Leon first. He's the shop manager and knows the whole shop.

For this task you will talk with someone to find out more about his or her job. You will read through a script on page 155 with a partner, then interview another person.

VISUALIZE THE WHOLE TASK

Think carefully about how you interact with people. • When you first get to know someone, what do you talk about? • How do you begin the conversation?

YOUR NOTES

How will you get to know more about Leon and his job? What will you say first? What questions could you ask?

I'll start the conversation by _____

_____

I'll ask Leon about _____

_____

Read the script on page 155. Ask your partner to read the part of Leon.

After you've read the script, interview someone to learn more about his or her job. Think of a job you're curious about. Make a plan to interview a person holding this job. Plan your steps below.

1. What job did you choose? _____

2. Who will you interview? _____

3. When will you talk with this person? _____

4. Why do you want to know about this job? _____

_____

5. Plan your first statement or introduction: _____

_____

6. What would you like to know about the person and job you've chosen? List several things below.

_____

_____

7. Is there something this person could show or teach you about the job? How could you ask? Write your ideas below.

_____

_____

8. Now complete your interview with the notes you've made above.

TASK RECAP

▶ Did you find someone to read the script on page 155 with you?
▶ In your interview, did you find out what you wanted to know about the job?

Now that you've interviewed someone about his or her job, how did it go? • Was any part of the interview awkward? • How would you change your questions next time?

_____

_____

Technology and Tools: An offset press operator most likely enjoys technology. To make sure each final document meets a high quality standard, the operator fine-tunes the press with computer and hand controls that affect every part of the press.

* You should do the Systems task on page 44 before beginning this task.

MAKE QUALITY CONTROL ADJUSTMENTS TO A PRESS

It's after lunch and you're setting the press for a large job. It's a brochure for a local realty company.

You've cleaned the ink rollers from the last job and mixed the ink for this job. You've checked the plate for imperfections and attached it to the plate cylinder. The paper stock is good: it's dry, warm, and flat. You've loaded it already.

As you run a sample and check it against the proof, this is what you see:

HOMELAND REALTY	HOMELAND REALTY
CAROL MIKOLIC	CAROL MIKOLIC
PRESIDENT	PRESIDENT
proof	sample

Some of the letters in the sample are over-inked.

For this task you'll need to make an adjustment to the press to correct this problem. You'll need to refer to the picture of the press on page 49.

VISUALIZE THE WHOLE TASK

Before you make the adjustment to the press, picture the task from beginning to end. • How will you find what caused the ink problem? • Where should you begin to look for a way to solve it? • What other information do you need to find a solution?

YOUR NOTES
What steps will you follow in adjusting the press?
First, I will _____
_____
_____

The press pictured above is shown in more detail on page 157. Study it carefully. Make sure you understand what each part of the press actually does and how each part affects the final document.

1. What do you think is creating the problem on the document?

_____

2. What part of the press will you adjust to correct the problem?

_____

3. On the diagram, mark the places where you will adjust the press to correct the problem.

TASK RECAP

▶ Double-check your three answers above. Do they match what you can tell from the diagram about the press?

What steps did you take to correct the performance of the press?

I monitored the product and noticed that the ink was _____

USE WHAT YOU'VE LEARNED

You have been learning a variety of skills within the context of being an offset press operator. Some of these skills are

▶ managing time
▶ preparing information
▶ understanding an organization's system
▶ talking with someone to find information
▶ adjusting machinery

1. Name two jobs that might require these skills. How might these skills be put to use?

    Example: *an auto mechanic needs to adjust machinery*

    _____

    _____

2. Is there anywhere else you've used these skills? Where?

    Example: *At church I'm on the fundraising committee. I need to manage time and schedule*

    the events correctly.

    _____

    _____

3. Now that you've completed the tasks in this lesson, think of two new tasks at work or at home that you might try. What are they?

    _____

    _____

    _____

    _____

■■■ TRANSPORTATION AND TRADE

In the transportation and trade industry, more than 1 million new jobs are expected to open by the year 2005. The job growth is due to changes in transportation and an increase in personal travel. Workers in this field create ways to move passengers or freight. They may transport things themselves, as pilots and truck drivers or they may arrange transportation for others, as travel agents and air traffic controllers.

SOME SKILLS YOU WILL PRACTICE IN THIS LESSON

▶ Collect Appropriate Resources
▶ Present Vacation Information
▶ Understand Agency Services and Billing
▶ Interview a Customer
▶ Complete a Confirmation Sheet

Travel agents work within the transportation and trade career cluster. They make travel plans that fit a customer's budget, schedule, and personal taste. They give advice to customers, gather information when it's requested, and make arrangements once customers have agreed on a travel plan. Travel agents are most effective if they have a basic knowledge of geography and experience as a traveler.

Travel agents must enjoy working with people. They must be comfortable using computers and finding information from various sources. Travel agents are often asked to research options for a customer, then sell the customer on the best package. In smaller agencies, a travel agent may perform reception and accounting duties. In larger agencies, those duties are not a part of an agent's daily routine.

SOME RELATED JOBS

reservation sales agent
flight attendant
ticket agent
tour guide or escort

A Day at the Agency

Just as you are finishing up the billing on the Michaels **account**, the phone rings.

"Good afternoon, Rapid Travel. Can I help you?" you answer.

"Hello, yes, I think you can help us. This is Velma Smith, and I need your help planning a vacation."

Your afternoon weariness disappears. You respond, "I'd be happy to help you, Ms. Smith. Planning vacations is my favorite job as a travel agent. Give me an idea of what you're looking for."

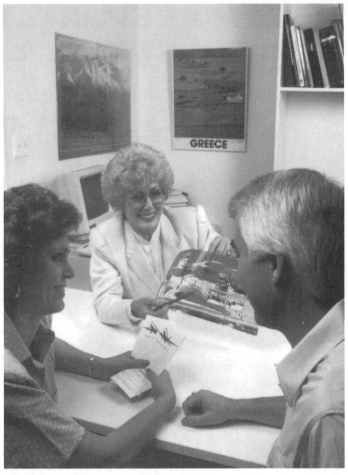

"Well, we've narrowed it down to Honolulu, Hawaii, or Disney World in Orlando, Florida. We haven't even decided when to go, but we have to go when our granddaughter wouldn't miss too much school. Raymond, my husband, doesn't want to be gone for more than a week. That's about all we've decided right now. I'm counting on you to give us more information."

"That's why I'm here. I can get information together for you on Hawaii and Disney World in minutes. I have brochures here in the office. Is that all you want right now, or would you like me to find out about airline flights, car rental, hotels, and sights to see?" you ask.

"Gosh, I hadn't thought about all that," Mrs. Smith replies. "I guess it makes sense to do all those things."

It sounds to you like this customer is getting a bit overwhelmed. You say, "I have a suggestion for you. Why don't we make an appointment right now for you to come in and we'll talk in person. I can show you some information and ask other questions then. Is Saturday at 10:00 A.M. good for you?"

"That's fine with me," Mrs. Smith agrees. "See you then."

You have your work cut out for you now. There are five major tasks ahead of you before the Smiths are content. You'll need to **collect appropriate resources** to help Mrs. Smith make some choices. You'll **present vacation information** to her. You will work to **understand agency services and billing**. You will **interview Mrs. Smith** in person. Finally, once the Smiths choose their travel plan, you'll **use technology to complete the confirmation sheet.**

SUMMARIZE THE TASKS

There are five tasks that you must accomplish in this lesson. These tasks are in **bold** type above. Below, write each task next to the correct category.

CATEGORY	TASK	ORDER	PAGE
Resources	*collect appropriate resources*	*2*	54
Information			57
Systems			60
Interpersonal	*interview Mrs. Smith*	*1*	62
Technology and Tools			64

PLAN YOUR TIME

Of the five tasks, are there some that should be done before others? *Hint:* Before you can complete the confirmation sheet, wouldn't you need to present information to Mrs. Smith? In the ORDER column above, number the tasks in the order you will complete them.

The page order of the tasks in this workbook is not necessarily the order in which you would do them. Follow the order you've decided above when you begin to work through the lesson.

THINK IT THROUGH

• What will you need to do these tasks? • What resources will you be gathering? • What other information do you need from Mrs. Smith? It's OK if you need more information at this point. You will find more information as you work through each task.

▶ Now go to the task listed as 1 and continue the lesson.

Resources: Travel agents use many resources, including brochures, pamphlets, books, and videos describing travel services. Agents must understand these resources and share them with customers as needed.

You should do the Interpersonal task on page 62 before beginning this task.

COLLECT APPROPRIATE RESOURCES

You've started to collect appropriate resources for Mrs. Smith. So far, you have several brochures about Hawaii and Disney World. But what else will you need to collect for her? Over the phone, she said that she'd like information on transportation, hotels, and points of interest.

Since you're located in Denver, Colorado, you know that the Smiths will be leaving from the Denver airport for their trip. You're not sure how much money they're going to spend on the vacation, so you should be looking for a variety of standards and costs for each service you research.

Rapid Travel has the following manuals and handbooks available:

Official Airline Guide (OAG) *North American Edition*
Official Airline Guide (OAG) Travel Planner: *Hotel and Motel Redbook*
Official Steamship Guide International
Official Hotel and Resort Guide: (OHRG) Volumes 1 to 4: *Worldwide Edition*
Official Hotel and Resort Guide: (OHRG) *Cruise Directory*
Hotel and Travel Index: *Worldwide*

For this task you will be collecting resources available both in and out of your office. You will make a phone call to collect some specific airline information.

VISUALIZE THE WHOLE TASK

Before you begin to collect the information you need, picture the task from beginning to end. • What resources do you already have in the office, and what will you need to find elsewhere? • Where could you find information that the office doesn't have on hand?

YOUR NOTES
How will you find all these resources? List the steps you will take.
First, I'll find out what's available in the office. Then, _____
_____
_____

Before you begin to collect resources, it's important to know what type of information you need. Then you can look for the resource that contains that type of information.

1.a. What information do you need to find for Mrs. Smith?

airline flight info _____

_____

_____

_____

_____

b. Which of these manuals might have that information?

OAG North American Edition _____

_____

_____

_____

_____

2.a. What information do you need that these manuals don't cover?

cost of plane tickets _____

_____

_____

b. How could you find this information?

I could call the airline _____

_____

_____

Your airline information search will go most smoothly if you know exactly what Mrs. Smith needs. Review the facts you gathered on page 52 during the interview with Mrs. Smith. Fill in the following information:

3. Length of vacation: _____

4. Price range of vacation: _____

5. Destination: _____

6. Number of people: _____

7. Now you have specific information. To complete your research, follow these steps:

Step 1   Choose a date for the Smith's vacation (*it should be one week long*):

_____ to _____

Step 2   Decide when the Smiths should travel (A.M. *or* P.M.?):

to destination: _____ from destination: _____

Step 3   Choose a national airline listed in your phone book:

airline: _____ phone: _____

Step 4   Use the information you've chosen to complete this question:
I need to know the price of a round-trip ticket from Denver, Colorado,

to _____. There will be ____ people flying, ____ adults
   (destination)

and ____ children, leaving on _____ in the ____ and returning
                  (date)   (time)

to Denver on _____ in the ____.
       (date)   (time)

Step 5   Place the call to the airline. Ask the question you completed in Step 4.
The price of one airline ticket is: $\underline{\$_____}$.

TASK RECAP

▶ Could you have found airline prices in one of the books in the office? Why or why not?

▶ Did you have all of the information you needed to get the ticket price?

REVIEW YOUR PLAN

Now that you've collected resources and information, what steps did you follow?

• What improvements could you have made in the steps?

_____

_____

Information: The age of information has changed all travel services. Travel agents must sort through vast amounts of information to find what is helpful to their clients. They must also communicate this information to the client.

PRESENT VACATION INFORMATION

For this task you will choose which information you'll present to Mrs. Smith. You will also decide exactly how to present the information. You will refer to the hotel descriptions on page 58.

You need to prepare a package for Mrs. Smith with a variety of travel options. You've begun by collecting information on some hotels in Hawaii. Here is the first one:

Closer to Waikiki, across Ala Moana Boulevard from the Ilikai, and equaling it in prime proximity to both the beach and the Ala Moana Shopping Center, is the Hawaii Dynasty Hotel, 1830 Ala Moana Blvd., Honolulu, HI 96815 (tel. 808 / 955-1111; reservations toll free 800 / 421-6662). Rising 17 stories, this 206-room resort is set well back from traffic noise, and since all rooms are air-conditioned, peace and quiet are doubly assured. There's a large pool and sundeck, a round-the-clock restaurant, and parking available. Rooms are regular size, but the bed sizes are deluxe. When you ask for twins, you get double beds. Closets, too, are big, and a smart vanitorium extends the whole length of the tub-and-shower-equipped bathroom. The rooms, nicely decorated, have color TV with in-room movies, air conditioning, and telephone; most have peeks at the ocean; some feature a lanai.

From April 16 to December 19, standard rooms are $55, deluxe are $60, superior/deluxe are $65, and suites, for up to four persons, are $150. Extra adults pay $12; there is no charge for children under 18 sharing their parents' room. From April 16 to December 19, there is a $15 per-day surcharge. AE, DC, MC, V. Parking $3.50 per day.

VISUALIZE THE WHOLE TASK

Before you present information to Mrs. Smith, picture the task from beginning to end. • How might you describe this hotel to Mrs. Smith? • If you present this hotel as one of her choices, what other types of hotels might you include? • How will you find out which hotel seems most appropriate for her?

YOUR NOTES
How will you present the hotel choices to Mrs. Smith?
First, I will read the entire description myself. Then, _____
_____
_____

Read the three descriptions of Hawaiian hotels below. Compare the descriptions. How are they alike? How do they differ?

As much a landmark on the Waikiki skyline as Diamond Head is the pink stucco Moorish-style hotel called the Royal Hawaiian, 2259 Kalakaua Ave., Honolulu, HI 96815 (tel. 808 / 923-7311; fax 808 / 924-7098; reservations toll free 800 / 325-3535). Standing on the site of King Kalanikapule's home by the sea of a century and half ago, it was Hawaii's original luxury hotel and has been the subject of newspaper and magazine stories, and the scene and site of scores of television shows and movies, since it opened back in 1927. Now under the Sheraton banner and with all its rooms, suites, and public areas recently redecorated and refurbished, the Royal Hawaiian wears its regal heritage like a proud mantle. You can't help saying, "They don't build hotels like this anymore."

Single or double rooms go from $210 (garden view) on up to $315 (ocean view). And all are beautiful, immense, and in the old style. Views are superb, and service is immediate and gracious. As you would expect, suites are splendid, priced from $380 up. You can stay either in the older, original six-story hotel building or in the new 17-story Tower wing, where all rooms overlook the pool and the Pacific. Guests at the Royal can use the food, beverage, and shopping facilities of the four other Sheraton resorts in Waikiki—the Sheraton Moana Surfrider, Sheraton-Waikiki, and the Princess Kaiulani—as well as the Sheraton Resort and Country Club in Makaha, and charge them to their bill. AE, MC, V. Valet parking $10 per day; self-park at Sheraton Waikiki, $5.

There's a very comfortable feeling about the Ambassador Hotel of Waikiki, 2040 Kuhio Ave.; Honolulu, HI 96815 (tel. 808 / 941-7777; fax 808 / 922-4579). It's neither too large nor too small, has a good location near the entrance to Waikiki, and the rooms are comfortable and attractive. All are done up in studio style, and they have air conditioning, telephone, and a sliding glass door opening onto a private lanai. The views are bigger and better in certain locations, those with higher price tags. Rates are $72 to $96 single, $80 to $104 double. We especially like the one-bedroom suites, which include full electric kitchen, and the corner suites with their great views of the ocean and Diamond Head. Here the price is $140 to $165 single or double; add $15 for an extra person. You can have breakfast, lunch, or dinner at the Cafe Ambassador, or drinks at the Embassy Bar, right on the premises. And if you're too lazy to walk to the Pacific, there's a large pool and sundeck lanai one floor above the bustle of Waikiki; drinks and snacks are at the ready, too. AE, CB, DC, JCB, MC, V. parking $3 per day.

The Pagoda Hotel, 1525 Rycroft St., Honolulu, HI 96814 (tel. 808 / 941-6611; fax 808 / 922-8061; reservations toll free 800 / 367-6060 from the U.S. and Canada), comes complete with a scenic floating restaurant on its premises. The 340-room complex is near the Ala Moana Shopping Center, which means about a 10-minute bus ride or drive to the heart of Waikiki. There are two swimming pools on the grounds. Two buildings face each other across Rycroft Street. One, called the hotel, has 200 newly renovated rooms with refrigerators; these run $75 moderate (floors 1 to 4), $85 deluxe (floors 5 to 12). The other building, called the Pagoda Terrace, has 160 kitchenette units; studios are $70, one-bedroom units for up to four people are $90, and two-bedroom suites for up to four are $105. Add $15 for an extra person in the room.

YOUR NOTES

_____

_____

_____

_____

_____

_____

_____

_____

_____

_____

_____

_____

_____

_____

_____

_____

_____

1. Fill in the chart below with the information you've found.

Category	Royal Hawaiian	Ambassador Hotel of Waikiki	Pagoda Hotel
cost (double room)			
features			
services			
recreation			
location			

To complete the task, first practice summarizing the information you've collected about each hotel listed in the chart above.

2. Next, try your plan out on someone you know. Ask a classmate or a friend to play the part of Mrs. Smith. Describe the hotels to this person. Ask which hotel he or she would choose.

TASK RECAP

▶ Did you find a difference in cost, services, and location among the three hotels?
▶ Did you describe the hotels clearly and concisely?

REVIEW YOUR PLAN

Now that you've practiced describing the hotels, how did it go? • Was it easy for your "client" to make a choice? • How might you improve your communication next time?

_____

_____

_____

Systems: Travel agents have to understand industry rules and regulations when purchasing an airline ticket, reserving a hotel room, and billing the supplier for commissions. An agent who knows these systems provides efficient customer service.

UNDERSTAND AGENCY SERVICES AND BILLING

Customers are not billed for your services. Suppliers, such as airlines, car rental companies, and hotels, pay travel agents a commission (or percentage) of the cost of the service.

You had planned a business trip for William Michaels from Denver to Washington, D.C. You booked his round-trip airfare, a hotel room for three nights, and a rental car for two of the three days. The car rental cost Mr. Michaels $89.54. Your commission from the rental service is 8%. So far, the Michaels bill looks like this:

Billing Information	Transportation Air/Ground	Accommodations Hotel/Motel	Meals B/L/D	Activity Car Rental
Cost	$823	$360		
% commission	9%	12%		
Amount billed	$74.07			
Total	$74.07			

For this task you will complete the billing statement above. You'll need to fill in the cost of the car rental, calculate commissions, and find the total amounts to be billed.

VISUALIZE THE WHOLE TASK

Before you complete the billing statement, picture the task from beginning to end.
• Where will you find the information to add to the chart? • How will you calculate the rest of the commissions owed to you? • What other service did you provide?

YOUR NOTES
How will you complete the billing statement? Which two commissions will you have to calculate? List your ideas.
First, I will fill in all the services I performed for Mr. Michaels. Then, I will calculate _____
_____
_____

Fill in the total cost of the services provided Mr. Michaels on the chart on page 60.

To calculate your commission, follow this formula:

$$\text{Total cost} \times \% \text{ commission} = \text{total commission}$$

$$\$823.00 \times .08 = \$74.07$$

Set up the equations to find the commission for these services:

1. Accommodations: _____ × _____ = $_____

2. Car Rental: _____ × _____ = $_____

3. Now solve the equations to find your commission amount. You may use a calculator if you'd like.

4. Finally, use your commission amounts to finish the Michaels bill on page 60. Be sure to complete the three columns fully.

TASK RECAP

▶ Did you enter information in the right place on the billing statement?
▶ Did you calculate your commission and the total amounts to be billed?
▶ Did you check your calculations?

The billing statement is complete. You have an idea of the commission you've earned for planning Mr. Michaels's trip. • Is it clear who pays an agent for services provided to customers? • What would you change next time you calculate your commissions?

_____

_____

_____

Interpersonal: A travel agent's most important job is providing services to clients. In order to provide appropriate services, the agent needs to spend time getting to know each customer.

INTERVIEW A CUSTOMER

Preparing for Mrs. Smith's visit is your first job. Whenever you interview a new customer, you follow this outline:

1. reason for trip, length of stay, number in party

2. destination and transportation desired

3. atmosphere desired (quiet, shopping, in city, beach, recreation)

4. accommodations: room category (single, double, any special needs)

5. price range for services

For this task you will ask your client questions about the vacation to get specific information.

VISUALIZE THE WHOLE TASK

Before you begin questioning Mrs. Smith, picture the task from beginning to end.
• What will you do first? • When are you planning to interview her? • What information do you need?

YOUR NOTES
How will you begin your conversation with Mrs. Smith? What questions will you ask her? Write down the steps you will take.
I will start by introducing myself and thanking her for coming. Then, I will confirm what she's already told me

Ask a classmate, teacher, friend, or family member to play the role of Mrs. Smith. Interview this person to find out more information about what Mrs. Smith is looking for in her vacation. *(The person you interview will make the choices for Mrs. Smith.)* Use the outline below to guide you as you ask questions.

Record the choices below. You will be using these choices elsewhere in this lesson.

1. Destination: (choose one) ____ Hawaii   ____ Disney World

2. Reason for trip: _____

3. Number of people: ____ adults   ____ children

4. Length of stay: _____

5. Transportation: air/ _____

      ground/ _____

6. Atmosphere: ____ casual   ____ elegant

7. Accommodations: _____

8. Price range:

    transportation: ____ low   ____ medium   ____ high

    accommodations: ____ low   ____ medium   ____ high

    recreation: ____ low   ____ medium   ____ high

TASK RECAP

▶ Did you ask all of the questions you needed to ask?
▶ Were you courteous?

How did the interview go? • Did you get all the information you needed? • Is there anything you'd change the next time you interview a customer?

_____

_____

Technology and Tools: A travel agent's most valuable tool is a computer. To access, change, verify, and review travel information, agents must know how to use a computer.

You should do the Interpersonal task on page 62 before beginning this task.

COMPLETE A CONFIRMATION SHEET

The person you chose to interview on page 63 has made some choices for the Smith family vacation. It's time for you to record those choices on a confirmation sheet. This sheet shows what you and the client have agreed upon—specific dates and times, flight numbers, and hotel rates.

Study the completed confirmation sheet below.

PASSENGERS		BUS PHONE	AGENT	DATE BOOKED	DATE DEPART	DATE RETURN		CASH PAID OUT		
William Michaels		753-7254	PR	6/9/93	7/11/93	7/14/93	DATE	AMOUNT	PAID TO
		HOME PHONE	BILL TO:							
		425-6004	Children's Hospital							
		BUS PHONE	ADDRESS					CASH RECEIVED		
			1056 E. 19th Ave.				DATE	AMOUNT	PAID TO
		HOME PHONE	Denver, CO 80219							

	FROM	TO	CARRIER	FLT	CLASS	DAY DATE	DEPART	ARRIVE	TOTAL COST			
A I R • B U S •	Denver	Wash. DC	DL	104	D	Su 7/11	4:00p	7:17p	823.00			
										NET COMMISSIONS		
H	DATE	HOTEL		CITY	NITES	ROOM	PLAN	RATE	DATE	AMOUNT	PAID TO
O T	7/11-14	K Marriot		Arlington	3	653	S	120.00			
E L											
• A	DATE	COMPANY		CITY	MAKE-MODEL	DROP OFF-TIME/PLACE		RATE			
U T O	7/12	Budget		Arlington	Mid-size	K Marriot		39.99			

For this task you will use a keyboard to fill out a blank confirmation sheet on the Smith family vacation. You will use the blank confirmation sheet on page 161.

Before you begin to fill out a confirmation sheet, picture the task from beginning to end. • How will you complete a confirmation sheet on Mrs. Smith? • Is there a computer or typewriter that you could access? • Do you have all the information you need from your interview? • Is there anything on the completed sheet on page 64 that you don't understand?

YOUR NOTES
What steps will you take to complete the confirmation sheet? Write them below. *I will make sure I understand the confirmation sheet. Then,* _____   _____   _____

COMPLETE THE TASK

1. Look at pages 159 and 161. They list specific information about air transportation, hotel accommodations, and car rental for trips to Hawaii and Disney World. If the person you interviewed did not pick specific dates and times, choose them yourself.

2. Now use the resource pages, the interview information, and any choices you may have made to complete the confirmation sheet on page 161. **Input** the data on a computer screen. If you prefer, pull page 161 from the book and place it in a typewriter to complete.

TASK RECAP

▶ Did you confirm airline, hotel, and car rental plans?
▶ Do your plans satisfy Mrs. Smith's wishes?

REVIEW YOUR PLAN

Now that you've completed the confirmation sheet, how did it go? • What steps did you take? • What problems did you have? • How would having the right technology have helped?

_____

_____

_____

USE WHAT YOU'VE LEARNED

You've been learning a variety of skills within the context of being a travel agent. Some of these skills are

- ▶ gathering resources
- ▶ communicating information
- ▶ understanding services and payment
- ▶ interviewing a customer
- ▶ inputting data on forms

1. Name two other jobs that might require these skills. How might these skills be put to use?

   Example: *a sales representative needs to gather resources before trying to make a sale*

   _____

   _____

2. Is there anywhere else you've used these skills? Where?

   Example: *at home I need to pay bills and understand the services I'm paying for*

   _____

   _____

3. Now that you have completed the tasks in this lesson, think of two new tasks at work or at home that you could try. What are they?

   _____

   _____

   _____

   _____

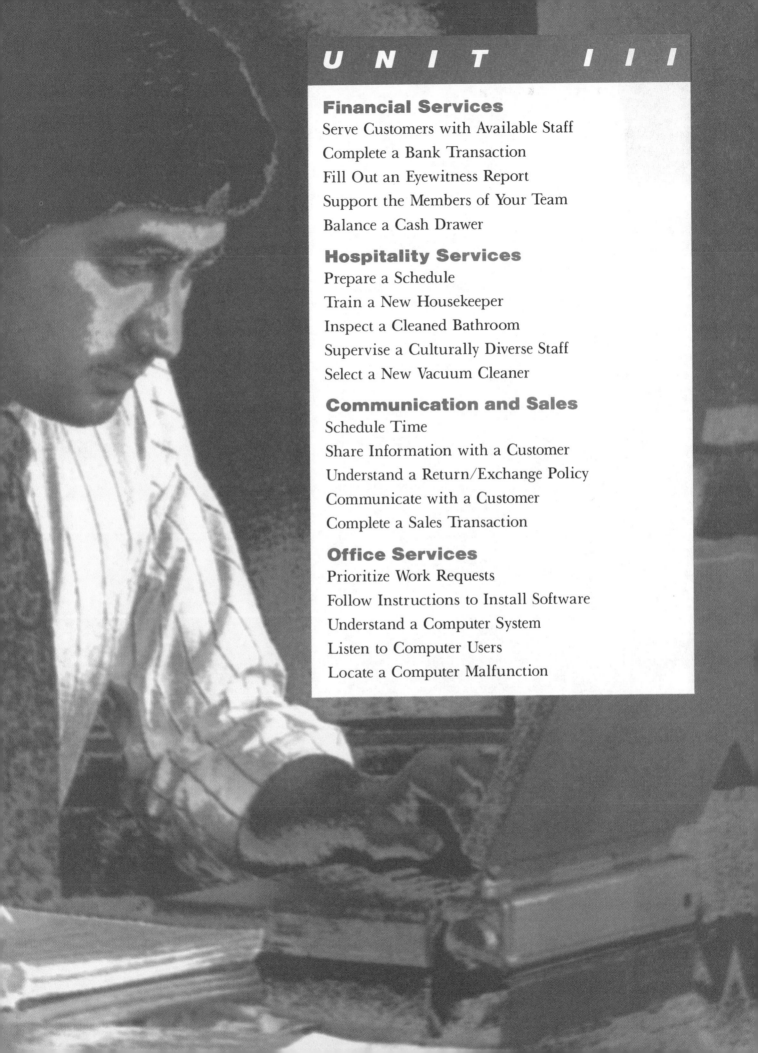

UNIT III

■■■ FINANCIAL SERVICES

The growth rate for jobs in the financial services industry is expected to be about the same as that for all jobs over the next ten years. Workers in the financial services field do high-level clerical work that requires special skills and knowledge. They help companies and other organizations keep track of accounts and business **transactions**. These workers collect, organize, compute, and record numerical information.

SOME SKILLS YOU WILL PRACTICE IN THIS LESSON

- ▶ Serve Customers with Available Staff
- ▶ Complete a Bank Transaction
- ▶ Fill Out an Eyewitness Report
- ▶ Support the Members of Your Team
- ▶ Balance a Cash Drawer

The financial services career cluster includes the job of bank teller. Bank tellers spend most of their time working with people. They serve diverse clients and customers by cashing checks, depositing money into accounts, and helping customers with other financial services.

When bank tellers aren't working with customers, they work to build their knowledge of banking services. With this knowledge, bank tellers can refer clients to the correct bank **representative** when needed. They become more valuable employees as they build skills and experience.

Bank tellers must feel as comfortable working with money as they do working with people. They buy and sell foreign currency, sell government bonds and **securities**, and balance funds. This requires knowledge of math and some accounting procedures.

SOME RELATED JOBS

cashier supervisor
head teller
accounting clerk

Banking on Skills

Monday is always busy at the downtown branch; today is no exception. Even you, the head teller, have worked as a teller all morning because of the number of customers in line. As the lunchtime rush approaches, you know that you won't be back to your regular duties soon.

Your thoughts are interrupted when you notice Javier, the teller next to you, leave his area and go talk to the security officer. He has customers in line. This isn't like him.

You walk quickly over to them and ask, "Is everything all right?"

Javier says, "No! That man in the black leather jacket just robbed me. He said he knew where my wife works, and he'd hurt her if I didn't cooperate with him," Javier replies, his hands shaking.

You look out the window. A man in a black leather jacket is racing off on a black motorcycle.

"Come with me now," you tell Javier. "Everything will be OK. Your wife won't be hurt. You did what he asked. Michelle will help you now, and the rest of us will cover the customers."

After you walk Javier over to Branch Manager Michelle Johnston's office, you quickly survey the bank lobby. The lines have grown. It seems that no one suspects a robbery has taken place. People are calmly but impatiently waiting in line. All eyes are on you as you think about reporting the robbery. You realize it will take a few minutes to figure out how to cover Javier's absence.

"Could I have your attention?" you ask the customers. "One of our tellers is not feeling well. I'd appreciate your patience for a few minutes while we make arrangements to cover for his absence. We will continue to serve customers momentarily."

You glance around, wondering how you'll help staff recover from the incident. You move toward Javier's teller area, quickly locking his cash drawer. "I'll have to balance that later," you think to yourself.

You must think quickly. There are quite a few customers, but you're shortstaffed. You must manage to **serve the customers with the staff that's available**. You will **complete bank transactions** for customers. The branch manager will report the robbery. When the police arrive, they'll want you to **fill out an eyewitness report**. You'll need to consider ways of **supporting your staff** to be sure they've recovered from the robbery. Finally, you'll need to **balance Javier's cash drawer** to count the losses.

SUMMARIZE THE TASKS

There are five tasks that you must accomplish in this lesson. These tasks are in **bold** type above. Below, write each task next to the correct category.

CATEGORY	TASK	ORDER	PAGE
Resources	_____	___	72
Information	_____	___	74
Systems	_____	___	76
Interpersonal	_____	___	78
Technology and Tools	_____	___	80

PLAN YOUR TIME

The five tasks listed above are only part of a bank teller's day. As you read through the narrative on page 70, you may have recognized a natural order the tasks might follow. Under the ORDER column above, list the tasks in the order you will complete them.

THINK IT THROUGH

You are very capable, but you will need help today. • What people will you need? • Are there resources you can access? • Can you think of any information you don't have now that you should locate?

▶ Now go to the task *you* listed as 1 and continue the lesson.

Resources: Each day's schedule is different for a bank teller. Some services take longer than others. Tellers are always balancing accuracy with speed. Customers take priority over **data tracking**, but customers also expect up-to-date information on a variety of services. This requires a bank teller to update records whenever possible.

SERVE CUSTOMERS WITH AVAILABLE STAFF

For this task you will plan how to organize the tellers and the customers to get through the bank's lunchtime rush. You will need to decide how to move the customers through the line as quickly as possible.

The police have arrived. Javier and Ms. Johnston will be busy for the next few hours. It is 12:15 P.M. and the lunch crowd is beginning to arrive. You have yourself, Summer (another teller), and Chris (a trainee) to handle all the customers. The assistant manager is available for opening new accounts and handling commercial accounts services, **investment** issues, and customer complaints.

Different tellers are qualified to make different transactions:

Window 1 *You*	Window 2 *Summer*	Window 3 *Chris*
deposits	check cashing	deposits
withdrawals	deposits	withdrawals
solve account problems	**withdrawals**	
fund **verification**	money orders	
provide account information		

VISUALIZE THE WHOLE TASK

Before you can organize the tellers and the customers, picture the task from beginning to end. • What can you do to accommodate the customers with the available staff? • How could you organize customers according to the services they need?

YOUR NOTES
How will you organize the lines so you can serve customers efficiently with a small staff? List the steps you will follow. _____ _____

The customers in line need these services:

▶ deposits and withdrawals (most people)
▶ account information (two people)
▶ money orders (two people)
▶ problems with accounts (three people)
▶ questions about a **certificate of deposit** investment (one person)

1. Complete the diagram below to show how you'd organize the tellers and the customers. List the services each teller will provide under the window.

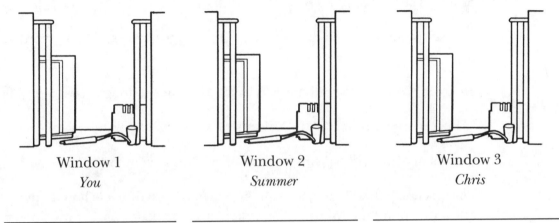

Window 1   Window 2   Window 3
You   *Summer*   *Chris*

_____   _____   _____

_____   _____   _____

_____   _____   _____

_____   _____   _____

2. How can you direct customers to certain lines? _____
_____

TASK RECAP

▶ Does your plan provide quick service to each customer?
▶ Are the customers evenly balanced across all three tellers?

Look back at your plan. • What steps did you follow? • How would you change your staff resources in the future?

_____

_____

Information: Bank tellers spend most of their time doing transactions such as cashing checks, making deposits and withdrawals, and issuing money orders and cashier's checks. They may do this face-to-face with customers or through night, **courier**, mail, or machine deposits.

COMPLETE A BANK TRANSACTION

After the robbery, you continue to serve customers at the teller's window. Your current customer, Mr. Nelson, has been waiting in line since the robbery. He sees the police arrive and is curious about what happened. You know, however, that bank policy restricts you from discussing robbery details with customers. Only the bank security officer is authorized to discuss these details.

Mr. Nelson hands you a deposit slip, cash, and two checks. These items are found on page 163.

He asks, "What happened here? Why are the lines so long? What are the police doing?"

"There's been a robbery, Mr. Nelson," you reply factually.

"A robbery!" he blurts. "Are we in danger? Was anyone hurt?"

For this task you will complete Mr. Nelson's transaction *and* handle these tough questions about the robbery. You will need a calculator and, if possible, a computer. You will need to be calm and courteous but you cannot discuss the details of the robbery.

Before you begin the transaction, picture the task from beginning to end. • What will you do first? • What other information or resources might you need?

YOUR NOTES
How will you answer Mr. Nelson's questions? Write an answer to each question below. "Are we in danger?" _____ "Was anyone hurt?" _____

1. Decide *when* you will answer Mr. Nelson's questions:

   ☐ before transaction   ☐ during transaction   ☐ after transaction

2. To complete Mr. Nelson's deposit, follow these steps:

   Step 1   Ask for identification and receive customer's savings account **deposit slip**, cash and/or check(s).

   ▶ Do you have all the items you need? If not, ask Mr. Nelson for the missing piece: _____

   Step 2   Use calculator to check accuracy of deposit slip.

   ▶ Is it correct? _____

ON THE CALCULATOR
(1)(0)(0)(·)(0)(0)
(+)(8)(6)(9)(·)(2)(3)
(+)(5)(0)(·)(0)(0)
(=)(_____)

   Step 3   Enter customer's account number and deposit amount onto your computer:

   ▶ Account number _____   ▶ Deposit amount _____

   Step 4   Place bank ticket and deposit slip into validator.

   Step 5   Place original bank ticket and carbon copy in sort box.

   Step 6   Print customer deposit receipt and give it to customer.

   Step 7   Give customer cash (if required) and thank customer.

   TASK RECAP

   ▶ Did you read through all seven steps?
   ▶ Did you answer Mr. Nelson's questions? When?

REVIEW YOUR PLAN

• How did the transaction go? • Was it difficult to do two things at once? • Why or why not?

_____

Systems: Bank tellers must understand many systems and procedures. There are computer systems, referral systems for customer service, and specific procedures for handling bank transactions and police reports.

FILL OUT AN EYEWITNESS REPORT

Javier has been talking with a bank security officer, the police, and the FBI for several hours. Now the police are ready to question other bank staff about what they saw during the robbery. You assume the police will ask what you remember about the robber. You did not see him, but you did see the motorcycle.

When they call you in for questioning, they are interested in more than you expected. They ask about Javier's behavior, the customers you were helping at the time of the robbery, and very specific information about the motorcycle. It seems you're the only person who got a good look at the motorcycle.

For this task you will complete an eyewitness report for the police.

Here is what you saw:

VISUALIZE THE WHOLE TASK

Before you begin the eyewitness report, think about the steps you'll take. • How will you remember details you saw for only a few seconds? • Why did the police ask about Javier's behavior? • How does your position as Javier's supervisor affect things?

YOUR NOTES
What steps will you take in describing the photo?
_____
_____

Study the photo on page 76. Then fill in details on each line below.

1. Driver: _____

2. Motorcycle: _____

3. Other details: _____

4. Now complete the Identification Report below. Include the details you've noted above. Since you are the only person who saw the robber leave, make your report as complete as possible. Consider everything.

IDENTIFICATION REPORT

Witness name:	Date:
Type of incident:	Location: MidTown Mutual Savings Bank
Description of incident:	
Witness signature:	Officer signature:

TASK RECAP

▶ Does your report contain all the details it should?
▶ Is your description well organized?

Now that you've completed the report, see how effective it is. Have a classmate or your instructor read the report *without looking at the photograph*. Ask whether this person has a picture in mind. Then show the motorcycle photograph to your partner. What does this person notice that you should add to your report?

_____

_____

Interpersonal: Bank tellers spend much of their time with customers. They also work as a team with other bank staff. They may help a co-worker, teach a trainee a specific skill, call staff at another branch office, or work with the branch staff to prepare for an audit.

SUPPORT THE MEMBERS OF YOUR TEAM

For this task you will practice supporting one of your co-workers (Summer or Chris) after a stressful day. You will make sure that your co-worker is not upset by the robbery. You'll need to find a partner to work with you.

As the last customer of the day leaves the bank, Ms. Johnston locks the door. The tellers each find a chair and talk about their stressful day. Javier has left early. He needed to put the robbery behind him and see his wife.

"This has been *some* day," Summer comments.

"No kidding," Chris responds. "You offer quite a training program."

You and Summer laugh. You say, "Let's hope we never have to experience another robbery. I hope Javier is all right."

As you listen to the tellers and banking staff, you realize all of the extras this day required of them. Everyone worked quickly and willingly without revealing any of the stress caused by the robbery. The staff handled themselves professionally. They did not breach security and they supported the police in the investigation. Most important, the staff supported Javier, who had followed bank policy during the robbery: never put anyone in danger, but observe and record information for the police.

Ms. Johnston comes out of her office. She asks, "Could everyone please come into my office for a quick debriefing with security officers?"

VISUALIZE THE WHOLE TASK

Before you begin talking with your co-workers, think about how you feel. • After a stressful day, are you calm enough to offer your support to others? • How can you show the staff your appreciation for the work they've done?

YOUR NOTES
How will you find out whether your co-worker is all right? In what ways can you offer praise for the good work he or she did?
_____
_____

To make sure your co-worker is not upset by the robbery, you'll need to ask some questions. Decide whether you'll talk to Summer or Chris. Then write at least one sentence or question for each area below.

1. Find out how your co-worker is doing:

   _____

   _____

2. Praise your co-worker for doing well under stress:

   _____

   _____

3. Point out that Javier handled the robbery correctly:

   _____

   _____

4. Give support to your co-worker for his or her teamwork:

   _____

   _____

5. Now ask your partner to play the part of either Summer or Chris. Explain how stressful the day has been for the bank tellers. Then, practice giving your support by using the sentences and questions written above.

TASK RECAP

> ▶ Is your co-worker OK?
> ▶ Did you remember to praise him or her *and* to point out Javier's good work?

How did your partner accept the support that was offered? • Did this person say or do anything you didn't expect? • Would you do anything differently next time?

_____

_____

_____

Technology and Tools: Bank tellers must understand how to use and perform basic maintenance on a branch bank computer, adding machine, copy machine, money order machine, calculator, coin machine, and network computer system for all branches.

BALANCE A CASH DRAWER

After the robbery, you had to find out how much cash had been stolen.

When you balance a cash drawer, you must use a balance sheet, a computer printout of daily transactions. You'll also need to count the money in the drawer. The final balance on the balance sheet and the amount of money in the drawer should be the same amount. Look at the top of the balance sheet below. The abbreviations are defined on the left.

		Time	Cash Bal	A#	With/A	Ty	Dep/A	Ty	Bal
Cash Bal:	cash balance								
A#:	account number	9:30am	8000.00						8000.00
With/A:	withdrawal amount								
Dep/A:	deposit amount	9:31	8000.00	0077412			1846.22	ch	8000.00
Ty:	type of money	9:40	8000.00	0084361	**1400.00**	**c**			6600.00
	c: cash								
	ch: check	9:53	6600.00	0141233	**300.00**	**c**	470.37	ch	6300.00
		9:59	6300.00	1004217			789.32	ch	6300.00

To work with a balance sheet, follow these steps:

Step 1   Locate cash balance on first transaction ($8,000 at 9:30 A.M.)

Step 2   For first cash (c) transaction, subtract the cash withdrawal amount or add the deposit amount to the beginning balance ($8,000 – $1,400.00 = $6,600.00).

Step 3   Record answer as the new cash balance on the right side of the balance sheet.

Step 4   Record new balance in Cash Balance column for next transaction (note where $6,600.00 is entered for next transaction on the left side of the balance sheet).

For this task you will use a calculator or an adding machine to balance Javier's cash drawer. You will need to use the balance sheet on page 165 to complete this task.

VISUALIZE THE WHOLE TASK

Before you begin working with the balance sheet, picture the task from beginning to end. • What steps will you take to balance the drawer? • What technology will you use?

COMPLETE THE TASK

You'll need to check the balance sheet cash transactions to find out how much cash the robber took. Read the first three transactions on the balance sheet on page 80.

At 9:31 A.M., a customer with account 0077412 deposited a check for $1,846.22. Javier recorded the check, but didn't add that check amount to his cash balance, since it was not cash.

1. What did the 9:40 A.M. customer do? _____

   Javier would subtract that withdrawal amount from his balance:
   $8,000.00 − $1,400.00 = $6,600.00

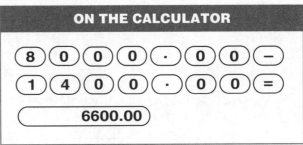

There is no cash left in Javier's drawer. To find out how much cash the robber took, you need to balance ONLY the *cash* transactions (shown in bold print on page 165).

2. What is the code for cash transactions? _____

Now turn to the balance sheet on page 165. Use a calculator or an adding machine to balance the cash transactions. Fill in both the right and left side balance columns after each transaction.

3. How much cash did the robber take? _____

TASK RECAP

▶ Did you work with cash transactions only—the ones marked *c*?
▶ Did you fill in the balance columns for each cash transaction?

REVIEW YOUR PLAN

Now that you've balanced the cash transactions, how did it go? • Are there any math skills you need to build? • If so, which ones? • Where can you find help with them?

USE WHAT YOU'VE LEARNED

You've been learning a variety of skills within the context of being a bank teller. Some of these skills are

- ▶ managing staff
- ▶ processing a transaction
- ▶ completing a report
- ▶ supporting other staff
- ▶ using technology to balance a cash drawer

1. Name two other jobs that might require these skills. How might these skills be put to use?

   Example: *a welder uses technology on the job when drilling holes at exact spots*

   _____

   _____

   _____

2. Is there anywhere else you've used these skills? Where?

   Example: *at school, I support my classmates after a hard day*

   _____

   _____

   _____

3. Now that you've completed the tasks in this lesson, can you think of two new tasks at work or at home that you might try? What are they?

   _____

   _____

   _____

   _____

■ ■ ■ HOSPITALITY SERVICES

The hospitality services industry is expected to grow at a faster rate than the average growth rate for all industries over the next decade. Many of these jobs will be entry level as other workers move into more highly skilled positions. Workers in this industry perform tasks such as cleaning, food preparation, operating simple machines, and personal services in hotels and motels.

SOME SKILLS YOU WILL PRACTICE IN THIS LESSON

▶ Prepare a Schedule
▶ Train a New Employee
▶ Inspect Someone's Work
▶ Supervise a Culturally Diverse Staff
▶ Select a New Tool

Housekeepers play a vital role in the hospitality industry. The head housekeeper is central to every hotel or motel. Head housekeepers supervise housekeepers. They make sure that rooms, hallways, and public areas are clean and neat. They also schedule staff, set cleanliness standards, and evaluate their housekeepers' performance.

SOME RELATED JOBS

custodian
personal attendant
caretaker
butler

Cleaning House

It's Saturday morning and you're on your way to work. Saturdays are always busy at the hotel. Guests sleep in, making it difficult for the housekeepers you supervise to begin cleaning right at 9:00 A.M. There are extra demands on your time: cleaning banquet rooms after Friday night and dealing with the usual Saturday staff shortage.

As you enter the hotel the bellhop greets you.

Violetta, the desk clerk, says, "Good morning. I suppose you're looking for the vacant ready report."

"Have you got it? It's going to be a crazy day," you reply.

"You're right about that. Here's the report and a note from personnel. Do you have a new housekeeper starting today?" Vi asks.

"Yes, a replacement for Elvia. I hope she's as good as Elvia was," you comment. "Is Franklin the manager today? I'd better see what else he has in store for me. Have a good morning, Vi. We'll be talking."

The phone is ringing as you open the door to the housekeeping office. "Housekeeping. Yes, here she is, Franklin," says Tuyet, handing you the phone.

"Good morning, Franklin," you say.

"Good morning to you. I know you have a busy day. Let me know if there's anything I can help you with. But I need your decision on that vacuum purchase today to get it ordered by Monday, OK?"

"OK, I'll find a few minutes this afternoon," you answer.

You have a busy day ahead of you. One of the first things you must do is **prepare a cleaning schedule**. You'll be sharing information as you **train a new housekeeper**. As usual, you'll **inspect room**s after they've been cleaned and **supervise a culturally diverse housekeeping staff**, many of whom are learning English. You'll also need to **select a new vacuum cleaner** for the hotel to purchase.

SUMMARIZE THE TASKS

There are five tasks you will accomplish in this lesson. They are in **bold** type above. Below, write each task next to the correct category.

CATEGORY	TASK	ORDER	PAGE
Resources	_____	____	86
Information	_____	____	88
Systems	_____	____	90
Interpersonal	_____	____	92
Technology and Tools	_____	____	94

PLAN YOUR TIME

How can you plan your time to do all these tasks? Are there some tasks that need to be done first, before other tasks can be done? Under the ORDER column above, list the tasks in the order you will complete them.

THINK IT THROUGH

• What resources will you need to do these tasks? • What information is already available? • What other people or information could be important?

▶ Now go to the task *you* listed as 1 and continue the lesson.

Resources: Hotel housekeepers must be good time managers. The rooms must be cleaned properly and on schedule. If rooms aren't ready for new guests to check into, the whole hotel schedule can be thrown off.

PREPARE A SCHEDULE

As head housekeeper, you need to plan the cleaning schedule before your staff can start working. You'll use these resources:

▶ the vacant ready report showing when each room can be cleaned
▶ the available cleaning staff

Based on these resources, you've come up with the following schedule for Saturday:

HEAD HOUSEKEEPING SCHEDULE   **DATE:** _____

Cleaning time
30 minutes/vacated room (v)
15 minutes/occupied room (o)

Staff	Caroline	Tanya	Tuyet	Tatiana	Head Housekeeper
8:30 A.M.	217	501	807 (o), 812 (o)		
9:00	222, 228	502 (o), 505, 511 (o)	827, 831		
10:00	230, 235, 237 (o)	520, 522, 548 (o)	840 (o), 842, 849		
11:15	break	break	break	break	break
11:30	239, 240	603, 610 (o), 612 (o)	903, 909		
12:30 P.M.	lunch	lunch	lunch	lunch	lunch
1:30	308, 321	618, 625	917 (o), 920, 922 (o)	Work with Tuyet	
2:30	336 (o), 342, 346	628 (o), 630, 641	928, 933, 940 (o)	↓	
3:45	break	break	break	break	break
4:00	403	700 (o), 703, 712 (o)	1001, 1019		
5:00	411	728 (o)	1027 (o)		
5:30	426	734 (o)	1039 (o)		

There's a problem today, though. Caroline has called in sick.

For this task you will rework the cleaning schedule. You'll need to decide who will clean Caroline's rooms. You'll also decide when and how you will complete your other tasks as head housekeeper:

- ▶ inspect eight clean rooms (15 minutes per room)
- ▶ begin to train a new housekeeper (about 2½ hours with you)
- ▶ select a new vacuum cleaner for the hotel (15 minutes)

VISUALIZE THE WHOLE TASK

Before you rework the schedule, picture the task from beginning to end. • How will you cover the rooms Caroline was scheduled to clean? • How will you schedule time for the tasks you must do?

YOUR NOTES
What ideas do you have for planning the day? List the steps you will follow.

COMPLETE THE TASK

Use the blank schedule on page 167 to rework your plan for the day. Caroline's rooms must be cleaned by someone else (Tanya, Tuyet, Tatiana, or you). You must plan time for your three other tasks as well.

TASK RECAP

- ▶ Is every room still scheduled to be cleaned?
- ▶ Did you give 15 minutes to occupied rooms, 30 minutes to vacant rooms?

REVIEW YOUR PLAN

Take a look at your schedule. • Did you plan the staff's time well? • Do you foresee any problems with the schedule?

Information: In a hotel, there is certain information that all housekeepers must know. The head housekeeper must find a different way to share this information if a housekeeper does not speak English.

TRAIN A NEW HOUSEKEEPER

Along with your other tasks today, you'll need to train your new employee, Tatiana. The regular training plan includes

- ▶ one hour of housekeeping instruction with you in a guest room
- ▶ ½ day observing another housekeeper clean rooms
- ▶ cleaning a room with a partner
- ▶ cleaning a room alone
- ▶ inspection of the room cleaned alone

Patricia from personnel arrives at the housekeeping office and introduces Tatiana.

"Hello, Tatiana. Welcome to the hotel," you say warmly.

Patricia leaves. You motion to Tatiana to have a seat. "Please sit down, Tatiana. How long have you been in the United States?"

"Three months," she says, looking down.

"Well, let's get started. Would you hand me the clipboard, please?" You point to the clipboard on the desk behind her.

Tatiana looks behind her, picks up a towel, and hands it to you. "No," you say, "the clipboard."

"Clipboard?" questions Tatiana.

For this task you must decide how to adjust your training plan to help Tatiana.

VISUALIZE THE WHOLE TASK

Before you begin training Tatiana, picture the task from beginning to end. • What special help will Tatiana need? • What can you do to help her?

YOUR NOTES
How will you adjust the training plan to help Tatiana? What steps will you follow?
_____
_____

Circle the options below that you'll use to train Tatiana. If you can think of another option, write it after *Other.*

Amount of Information: how to clean whole room   part of room

Training Time: lengthen   leave as usual

Language: English only   Russian only   use both languages

Communication: talk   show   read   write

Other:

Now finish your plan. Choose two options you circled above and list them below. Then describe why you think that option may be helpful to Tatiana.

1. Amount of Information: *train her to clean part of room*

   Why? *If I train her to clean bathrooms only today, it may be easier for her to learn the English terms needed.*

2. Training Time: _____

   Why? _____

3. Language: _____

   Why? _____

4. Communication: _____

   Why? _____

5. Other: _____

   Why? _____

TASK RECAP

▶ Did you keep in mind that Tatiana speaks little English?
▶ Did you describe why your choices will help Tatiana?

REVIEW YOUR PLAN

What steps did you follow to communicate with Tatiana? • What would you change the next time you try it?

_____

_____

Systems: A head housekeeper must work within the hotel's system. Before the front desk clerk can send a guest to a room, that room must be clean. The system created to inspect, correct, and approve clean rooms for guests must be well understood by all housekeeping staff.

INSPECT A CLEANED BATHROOM

It's your job to inspect cleaned rooms. You need to be sure that the hotel's cleanliness standards are met or exceeded. One of your housekeepers seems to have trouble when it comes to restocking the bathroom. She cleans the bathroom well, but she misplaces the new soaps, forgets the shower cap, or miscounts the clean towels.

For this task you will inspect a bathroom to be sure it's been cleaned and restocked correctly. You will compare how everything should look with the way they actually look.

VISUALIZE THE WHOLE TASK

Before you begin, picture the task from beginning to end. • What is the purpose for your inspection? • What are you specifically looking for in this bathroom? Why?

YOUR NOTES

What are you looking for when you inspect the bathroom? How will you teach the housekeeper and encourage her if there's a problem?

_____

_____

COMPLETE THE TASK

You've almost finished your inspection checklist. You need to check the towels and the bathroom tray. The illustration below shows the standard tray and towels.

bathroom tray

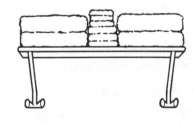
towel rack

Here is what the tray and towels look like in this bathroom.

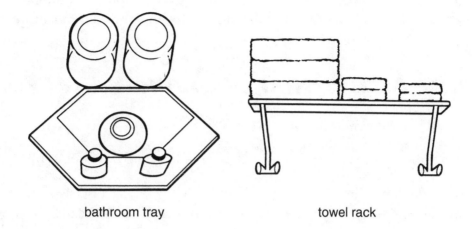

bathroom tray   towel rack

Is this acceptable? Why or why not? Below, write your reasons for accepting or rejecting this housekeeper's work. Also write how you plan to have this work corrected. It might seem tempting to simply correct the problem yourself, but that won't prevent it from happening again.

1. Reasons for accepting or rejecting:

_____

_____

2. Plan for correcting the work:

_____

_____

TASK RECAP

▶ Did you locate the problems with the restocking?
▶ Did you try to encourage your housekeeper to do better?

REVIEW YOUR PLAN

Review your inspection. • Did you do anything differently than you'd expected? • What changes would you make next time?

_____

_____

Interpersonal: Hotels and motels have always been places where a wide variety of people meet. Housekeepers deal with diverse groups of people, including their staff and their guests. They must be open-minded and respectful of different cultures and traditions.

SUPERVISE A CULTURALLY DIVERSE STAFF

"How is Tatiana working out?" Tuyet asks.

"She doesn't speak much English, but she's learning fast," you reply.

"Do you think she'll fit in? Is she friendly or shy?" Tuyet persists. "Elvia was such a good worker and fun, too. I hope Tatiana is as fun, and that she can cook as well as Elvia. I liked sharing her lunch."

"Tuyet," you say quickly, "you need to give Tatiana a chance to breathe. It's only her first day, and you're already sharing her lunch."

Tuyet's curiosity makes you think. Each one of your housekeepers is very different: Tuyet is from Vietnam, Tanya is from Eastern Europe, Caroline is an American-born teen parent, and now there's Tatiana from Russia.

For this task you will consider how you can welcome Tatiana to your housekeeping team. You want to encourage her to feel comfortable with the staff, but you don't want to overwhelm her on the first day. You will also interview someone to get their ideas.

VISUALIZE THE WHOLE TASK

Think through the steps you could take to include Tatiana as a part of the houskeeping team. • How can you create an atmosphere for staff members to get to know each other?

YOUR NOTES
List your ideas about welcoming Tatiana to your staff.
_____
_____
_____
_____

1. The list below has some ideas about welcoming Tatiana. Add your ideas to the list. What can you do? What can other staff members do?

   take Tatiana on a tour of the hotel

   assign pairs to work together

   introduce her to other hotel staff

   _____

   _____

   _____

   _____

Now find out what another person would do in this situation. Interview a classmate, friend, or family member. Ask the following questions:

2. What special steps would you take to help a new co-worker feel welcome?

   _____

   _____

3. How can you build teamwork among staff?

   _____

   _____

TASK RECAP

▶ Did you add ideas of your own to the list above?
▶ Did you ask the interview questions clearly and record the answers?

REVIEW YOUR PLAN

Did your interviews help you get ideas? • How would you help a new employee next time?

   _____

   _____

Technology and Tools: Head housekeepers help choose the technology and tools housekeepers use. Large hotels need different machines to clean floors, woodwork, carpet, and linoleum. Head housekeepers have experience with these tools. They help make decisions about new purchases.

SELECT A NEW VACUUM CLEANER

The hotel's vacuum cleaners are wearing out. Because the vacuum cleaners are used constantly, it is better to have dependable, working vacuums than to wait until a vacuum is beyond repair. You've been asked to choose a replacement model. You've talked with the sales representatives and read the specification sheets. You've narrowed the choice down to two models.

The day is getting shorter. Franklin, today's manager, needs your decision this afternoon.

For this task you will choose which vacuum cleaner to order for the hotel. You'll check for certain features you want in a vacuum cleaner. You will compare the specification sheets of two models found on page 169.

VISUALIZE THE WHOLE TASK

Before you choose a vacuum cleaner, picture the task from beginning to end. • Have you ever compared product information when making a purchase? • How much time do you think it will take you?

YOUR NOTES

How will you choose a vacuum cleaner? List the steps you will take.

_____

_____

COMPLETE THE TASK

When you compare the two models, you find some similarities:

▶ both models are made by dependable companies
▶ both have one-year **warranties**
▶ both have the same price
▶ your service shop can fix both models

You want to compare the features on the chart on page 95 as well.

Features	Riccar Model 2200	Panasonic MC-6217
weight/portability	*15 lbs*	*15 lbs*
adjust to different heights?		
various handle positions		
dust capacity		
cord length and release		
metal brushes		
filter system		
edge cleaning		
motor size		
optional tools		
headlight		
other		

1. Use the specification sheets on page169 to compare the features listed in the chart. Fill in the chart with this information. If you want to compare anything not listed on the chart, fill in the *other* row. When you're finished, answer this question:

2. What vacuum cleaner do you recommend the hotel purchase?

_____

3. Why? _____

TASK RECAP

▶ Did you compare the Riccar Model 2200 and the Panasonic MC-6217?
▶ Did you find all the information on the specification sheets?

REVIEW YOUR PLAN

Now that you've chosen a vacuum cleaner, what was difficult about the decision? • What was easy?

_____

_____

_____

USE WHAT YOU'VE LEARNED

You have been learning a variety of skills within the context of being a head housekeeper. Some of these skills are

- ▶ scheduling time
- ▶ communicating information
- ▶ inspecting and correcting performance
- ▶ interacting with others
- ▶ selecting appropriate tools

1. Name two other jobs that might require these skills. How might these skills be put to use?

   Example: _a bus driver communicates information by explaining a bus route to a passenger_

   _____

   _____

2. Is there anywhere else you've used these skills? Where?

   Example: _when my son cleans his room, I inspect it to be sure he's made his bed_

   _____

   _____

3. Now that you've completed the tasks in this lesson, can you think of two new tasks at work or at home that you might try? What are they?

   _____

   _____

   _____

   _____

■■■COMMUNICATION AND SALES

The growth rate for jobs in the communication and sales field is expected to be about the same as that for all jobs. This growth depends on the growth of the retail and service industries. Workers in this field deal with the public almost constantly. They provide a variety of services such as waiting on customers and accepting payment for purchases or services.

SOME SKILLS YOU WILL PRACTICE IN THIS LESSON

▶ Schedule Time
▶ Share Information
▶ Understand Store Policies
▶ Communicate with Customers
▶ Complete a Sales Transaction

Customer service representatives are part of the communication and sales industry. They help customers with problems they may have when doing business with a company. Customer service reps can be found in most places where products are sold: for instance, retail stores, manufacturing plants, wholesale showrooms, and distribution centers.

Customer service representatives respond to customer inquiries. They give product information—including technical facts, prices, and shipping time—and perform account transactions. They handle customer complaints, exchanges, and adjustments.

SOME RELATED JOBS

sales associate
telemarketing representative
order taker
equipment technician

Making an Exchange

Clyde and Shirley Mueller got up at 5:00 this morning to make the four-hour drive into the city. They plan to visit their children and return a gift.

"Did you remember to put the barbecue grill in the pickup?" Shirley reminds Clyde. "We don't need another wasted trip like last time."

"Enough talk about last time," snarls Clyde. "You're the one who covered the barbecue grill with the rug so I couldn't see it in the garage."

"OK. I just hope we don't argue in front of the kids for the next two days," Shirley mutters. "Of course, they'll probably be mad that we're returning the barbecue grill anyway. We'll all be fighting by the end of this trip."

You, on the other hand, didn't rise at 5:00 A.M. In fact, you were up late last night, and you aren't your usual energetic self. As you finish the paperwork on a special order taken yesterday, you overhear some arguing. Looking up, you see a couple pulling a barbecue grill through the front doors. They seem upset.

A customer service representative's days are unpredictable, but some tasks are the same from day to day. You must **schedule time** to get your work done. You'll need to **share information** with customers to help them make a purchase, then you'll need to **understand store policies** to ring up the transaction. You'll **communicate with customers** to find out what they need. Finally, you will **complete a transaction** on a cash register.

SUMMARIZE THE TASKS

There are five tasks you will accomplish in this lesson. They are in **bold** type above. Below, write the tasks next to the correct category.

CATEGORY	TASK	ORDER	PAGE
Resources	*schedule time*	*1*	100
Information			102
Systems			104
Interpersonal			106
Technology and Tools			108

PLAN YOUR TIME

In what order will you do these tasks? (*Hint:* For this lesson you should do the Resources task on page 100 first.) Under the ORDER column above, list the tasks in the order you will complete them.

THINK IT THROUGH

• What resources will you need to do these tasks? • What information?

▶ Now go to the task listed as 1 and continue the lesson.

Resources: Much of a customer service representative's work is responding to customer needs. Each day is **unpredictable** and can be hard to schedule. Managing time by setting goals and prioritizing is vital in this job.

SCHEDULE TIME

When you arrive at work, you don't know how many customers you'll see today *or* what they'll need. Helping customers is always your first priority. You'll need to allow yourself time to solve customers' problems. Throughout the day, you have other tasks as well:

- ► tracking long-term problems
- ► learning about new products
- ► processing paperwork
- ► filling in where the store needs you

To schedule your time, you need to:

- ► Preview and prioritize each day's tasks.
- ► Estimate the time tasks will take based on your work speed and the complexity of the tasks.
- ► Stay flexible and adjust the schedule as needed.
- ► Keep track of your progress as you complete tasks.

For this task you will schedule the time you'll need to finish this lesson. You will follow the steps above to plan when you'll do the other tasks in this lesson.

VISUALIZE THE WHOLE TASK

Before you begin to schedule your time, picture the task from beginning to end. Look over the tasks you wrote on page 99. • How will you prioritize? • Which task will be most important?

YOUR NOTES
List the steps you will take to plan your schedule.
_____
_____

COMPLETE THE TASK

Your goal will be to complete this lesson in the time you've planned for it—not too quickly or too slowly. To plan your lesson schedule, follow the steps on page 101.

Step 1 Preview each task in this lesson to see what you'll be doing.

Step 2 Prioritize each task (do you still agree with the order you decided on page 99?). List the tasks in the order you chose on the schedule below.

Step 3 Consider time. When do you think you'll complete each task? What might go quickly? Slowly? How much time will you need? List when you plan to complete each task and the time you'll need on the chart below.

Step 4 Keep track of your progress. How will you know that you've made progress?

Step 5 Build in time to be flexible. Change the schedule below if necessary.

Lesson Schedule

Task	Completed by (date/time)	Time Needed
1. *schedule time*		
2.		
3.		
4.		
5.		

TASK RECAP

▶ Did you prioritize the tasks in the lesson?
▶ Did you fill out the schedule completely?

REVIEW YOUR PLAN

Now that you've completed the lesson schedule, finish the rest of the lesson. Come back to this when you've finished and then answer the next two questions. • Did you stay on schedule? • How would you schedule things differently next time?

_____

_____

Information: Customer service representatives must share product and service information with customers. Customer service reps listen to the customer, ask questions, then choose information to fit the customer's needs.

You should do the Resources task on page 100 before beginning this task.

SHARE INFORMATION WITH A CUSTOMER

Standing at the customer service desk, you see two customers approaching. A salesperson is pushing a large barbecue grill box behind them.

"These are the Muellers. They want to return this barbecue grill," she says.

You turn to the Muellers and say, "That's a wonderful barbecue grill, one of our bestselling models. How can I help you today?"

Clyde responds. "We don't like this barbecue grill our kids gave us. We're getting too old to stand outside, waiting forever for the food to cook. And it's too big. We never cook this much just for us."

Shirley adds quickly, "We appreciate the thought, but it really isn't useful. I hope this return doesn't hurt the kids' feelings."

It's your job to keep the customers satisfied. However, the store asks that you try to exchange items rather than accept a return.

For this task you will try to exchange the Muellers' barbecue grill for another appliance. You will listen to the Muellers to find out their needs. Then, you will describe one product's features to a partner.

VISUALIZE THE WHOLE TASK

Before you begin the exchange, picture the task from beginning to end. • How can you find out what item the Muellers may need? • Who will you use as a partner to describe product information to?

YOUR NOTES
What steps will you take to satisfy the Muellers? List your ideas below.
_____
_____

There are two steps to this task:

► finding out what the Muellers may need
► sharing product information to make a sale

Read over what the Muellers said on page 102. Answer these questions:

1. What do they dislike about the barbecue grill? _____

_____

2. What can you guess about their needs? *they want to stay inside,* _____

_____

3. What other appliances might fit the Muellers' needs?

Appliance	Why?	Why not?
smaller barbecue grill		
toaster oven		
table top gas grill		
microwave oven		

4. Choose one product from the chart to recommend to the Muellers. Describe the product to your partner *as if he or she were a customer at your store.*

TASK RECAP

► Did you cover all of the information when you described the product?
► Did you speak slowly and carefully?

Was your presentation a success? • Were there any questions? • Did you sell it?

_____

_____

_____

Systems: The customer service representative is one of the first employees a customer will come to with a problem. Customer service reps aren't expected to know everything about a product, but they are expected to know their store's policies. They need to guide customers to the correct people, resources, and information.

You should do the Resources task on page 100 before beginning this task.

UNDERSTAND A RETURN/EXCHANGE POLICY

"Well, Mr. and Mrs. Mueller, have you made a decision? Would you like to exchange the barbecue grill for the microwave oven?" you ask.

"Shirley, I know you won't agree, but let's get the microwave oven," says Clyde.

"What makes you think I won't agree?" Shirley begins. "I usually do."

Wandering away, Clyde turns and says, "Start the paperwork."

For this task you will check to be sure the barbecue grill exchange fits your store's exchange policy limits. You will analyze the receipt for the barbecue grill. You'll also begin the paperwork to exchange the barbecue grill for the microwave oven.

Your store policy:

items must be returned within 30 days of purchase

receipt must accompany item, or store sticker must be evident

item must be in good condition or defect must be described in detail

reason for return must be in writing

exchange of merchandise is available

2959524	SHIPPING CODE	DIVISION 26	SALES NO. 406	SALES DATE	SELLING STORE NO. 406

| SC/CLC 0 | CASH 1 | COD 2 | DC 3 | MCA 5 | SCRCR 6 | EP/MCP 7 | | DELAY BILL DATE MONTH | DAY | CODE | DEF | PMT MONTH |

ACCOUNT NUMBER 9833 391 266 994   APPROVAL

NAME (PRINT) Clyde and Shirley Mueller

ADDRESS P.O. Box 72

CITY Tunica   STATE MS   ZIP CODE 38676   PHONE 555-0437

| DELIVERY DATE | MO. | DAY | ROUTE NO. | TYPE DEL. | HANDLING CODE | AREA CODE |

SHIP FROM
☐ STORE STOCK ☐ STORE WHSE.
☐ C.M.D.C. ☐ DIST. CTR.

SPECIAL INSTRUCTIONS

QTY.	STOCK NO/ MISC ACCT	DESCRIPTION	REGULAR PRICE	SELLING REDUCTION	SELLING PRICE
1	204498	Barbecue Grill	189.95	9.96	179.99

```
        406   EMP
983391266994  ACCT
         26   DIV
         99   MDSE
     179.99   EA

     7.900%   TAX
  2062   4069001
```

Randall Mueller
PURCHASED BY

```
179.99 + *
179.99 + S
 14.22 + T
194.21 + T
```

VISUALIZE THE WHOLE TASK

Before you begin the exchange, picture the task from beginning to end. • Do you have all the information you need? • What will you do first?

List the steps you plan to follow as you process the exchange.

_____

_____

COMPLETE THE TASK

Using information from the receipt on page 104, complete as much as you can of the return/exchange form below.

2959524	SHIPPING CODE	DIVISION	SALES NO.	SALES DATE	SELLING STORE NO.

SC/CLC 0	CASH 1	COD 2	DC 3	MCA 5	SCRCP 6	EP/MCP 7			DELAY BILL DATE			DEF	PMT
									MONTH	DAY	CODE		MONTH

ACCOUNT NUMBER _____ **APPROVAL**

NAME (PRINT) _____

ADDRESS _____

CITY	STATE	ZIP CODE	PHONE

DELIVERY DATE ♦	MO.	DAY	ROUTE NO. ♦	TYPE DEL. ♦	HANDLING CODE ♦	AREA CODE

SHIP FROM — REASON FOR RETURN

☐ STORE STOCK ☐ STORE WHSE.
☐ C.M.D.C. ☐ DIST. CTR.

QTY.	STOCK NO/ MISC ACCT	DESCRIPTION	REGULAR PRICE	SELLING REDUCTION	SELLING PRICE
			SALES TAX 7.9% ♦		
			DEPOSIT ♦		
PURCHASED BY			BALANCE ♦		

TASK RECAP

▶ Did you check to be sure the exchange fit company policy?
▶ Did you complete as much of the form as you could?

REVIEW YOUR PLAN

What steps did you follow to complete the return/exchange paperwork? • What information did you use? • What is still needed?

_____

_____

Interpersonal: Customer service representatives must work well with people. They need to listen carefully to understand and identify customers' needs. They need to suggest merchandise to fit those needs. Representatives must treat customers with courtesy, respect, and sensitivity to their ethnic, social, and educational backgrounds.

You should do the Resources task on page 100 before you begin this task.

COMMUNICATE WITH A CUSTOMER

Imagine you're standing at the service desk. The Muellers approach. The salesperson with them says loudly, "These people don't like this barbecue grill their kids gave them." The Muellers look surprised.

"What?" you ask. "How can someone not like a barbecue grill, especially as a gift? I guess your kids got it wrong, huh?"

Mr. Mueller responds, "Well, we don't like to barbecue that much."

"Don't like to barbecue?" you ask. "Impossible. Everyone likes it. It's the best way to cook," you say, turning your back to answer the phone.

Five minutes later, after hanging up the phone, you turn to the Muellers, who are still waiting at the desk. You say, "So what do you want to do about it? Return? Exchange? I have lots of forms to fill out and my head hurts."

The Muellers are a bit overwhelmed. They say, "Return."

For this task you will analyze the conversation above. You will pinpoint the remarks that could have offended the Muellers and rewrite the conversation to avoid the problems above. Finally, you will practice your new conversation with a partner.

VISUALIZE THE WHOLE TASK

Before you begin the task, picture it from beginning to end. • How does the gruff treatment make the Muellers feel? • What do you need to do differently?

YOUR NOTES
What will you say to the Muellers? What will you try to avoid?
_____
_____

Begin this task by analyzing the conversation on page 106. Clearly, the Muellers aren't satisfied with your service. How can you change that? Find at least five points in the conversation that may have offended the Muellers. Write those points below.

1. *"These people don't like this barbecue grill their kids gave them."*

   What's wrong? *The statement doesn't seem respectful to the Muellers or to their kids.*

2. _____

   What's wrong? _____

3. _____

   What's wrong? _____

4. _____

   What's wrong? _____

5. _____

   What's wrong? _____

6. Now rewrite the conversation with the Muellers on a blank sheet of paper. Correct each point that was offensive in the original conversation, but cover the same amount of information.

7. When your conversation is complete, practice it with a partner. Have a friend, classmate, or family member read the part of the Muellers. You should read the parts of the employees. Have your partner check your work to see if you showed the Muellers courtesy, respect, and helpfulness.

TASK RECAP

   ▶ Did you pinpoint what was wrong with the original conversation?
   ▶ Did you read your new conversation with a partner?

Was your new conversation a success? • How would you change it next time?

_____

_____

Technology and Tools: Customer service representatives use cash registers to complete transactions. Employers offer training on their specific systems.

*You should do the Resources task on page 100 before beginning this task.

COMPLETE A SALES TRANSACTION

The Muellers have decided to exchange the barbecue for a microwave oven.

For this task you will complete the Muellers' exchange. You'll enter the return, the exchange, and the money amounts onto a cash register. You will refer to their sales receipt on page 104.

This is the cash register keyboard you'll work with.

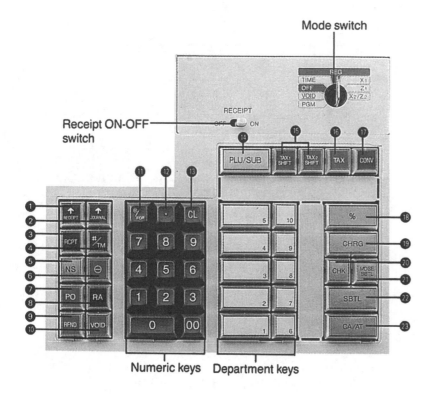

Mode switch

Receipt ON-OFF switch

Numeric keys   Department keys

❶ Receipt paper feed key
❷ Journal paper feed key
❸ Receipt issue key
❹ Non-add/time display key
❺ No-sale key
❻ Discount key
❼ Paid-out key
❽ Received-on-account key
❾ Refund key
❿ Void key
⓫ Multiplication/split-pricing key
⓬ Decimal point key
⓭ Clear key
⓮ Price look up/sub-department key
⓯ Tax 1 and tax 2 shift keys
⓰ Tax key
⓱ Conversion key (for currency conversion)
⓲ Percent key
⓳ Charge key
⓴ Check key
㉑ Merchandise subtotal key
㉒ Subtotal key
㉓ Cash/amount tendered key

Mode switch
REG: For entering sales
TIME: Allows time display
OFF: Prevents key entry
VOID: Cancellation after the finish of transaction
PGM: Programming
X1:   Reading daily totals
Z1:   Resetting daily totals
X2/Z2: Reading and resetting periodic totals

VISUALIZE THE WHOLE TASK

Before you complete the transaction, picture the task from beginning to end. • Why should you record the return before you write up the exchange? • What resources and information will you use?

YOUR NOTES

How will you handle the Muellers' exchange?

First, I will _____

_____

_____

COMPLETE THE TASK

Complete the Muellers' exchange on the cash register on page 108 or use a real one. *Use the CL key to clear mistakes.* Follow these steps:

Step 1 Turn register on to enter sales.
Step 2 Enter refund amount for barbecue grill.
Step 3 Push department #9.
Step 4 Push refund key.
Step 5 Enter new sale amount for microwave oven.
Step 6 Push department #2.
Step 7 Push merchandise subtotal key.
Step 8 Push tax key.

The Muellers owe $19.96 for the cost difference. They pay cash.

Step 9 Count the money; push cash/amount tendered key.
Step 10 Put the money in the register drawer. Push receipt issue key.
Step 11 Give register receipt and exchange form to the Muellers.

TASK RECAP

▶ Did you find all the keys you needed on the cash register?
▶ Did each of the steps above make sense to you?

REVIEW YOUR PLAN

Now that you've completed a sales exchange, how did it go? • What might you do differently?

_____

_____

USE WHAT YOU'VE LEARNED

You've been learning a variety of skills within the context of being a customer service representative. Some of these skills are

- ▶ scheduling your time
- ▶ finding and explaining information
- ▶ understanding policies
- ▶ being respectful of others
- ▶ operating technology

1. Name two other jobs that might require these skills. How will you put these skills to use?

   Example: *a receptionist finds and explains information for people*

   _____

   _____

   _____

2. Is there anywhere else you've used these skills? Where?

   Example: *at home I am respectful of my wheelchair-bound neighbor*

   _____

   _____

   _____

3. Now that you've completed the tasks in this lesson, can you think of two new tasks at work or at home that you might try? What are they?

   _____

   _____

   _____

   _____

■■■OFFICE SERVICES

The office services industry is expected to have a higher growth rate than the average rate of growth for all jobs by the year 2005. Workers in this field perform administrative tasks needed to keep organizations running smoothly. They may do clerical tasks as word processors and receptionists. They also operate and repair computers that type, print, sort, compute, receive, and send information. Some of these workers may give technical support and training to computer users.

SOME SKILLS YOU WILL PRACTICE IN THIS LESSON

▶ Prioritize Work Requests
▶ Follow Instructions to Install Software
▶ Understand a Computer System
▶ Listen to Computer Users
▶ Locate a Computer Malfunction

One career within the office services industry is computer support specialist. These specialists help computer users get the most from their equipment. They give technical support, training, and suggestions for system improvements. Computer support specialists must know how computers work and how to program computers. They should know about hardware and software programs. They should be able to analyze business needs and match those needs to the right computer systems.

Computer support specialists install computers, related equipment, and software programs. They find software and hardware problems and make minor repairs. They may also write computer programs for customers.

SOME RELATED JOBS

computer service technician
computer operator
computer programmer
systems analyst

Expert Advice

As you enter the YMCA this morning, the line at the reception desk is long. People are checking in to exercise, to pay their monthly membership fee, and to attend a workshop. One person asks what it costs to spend a couple of nights there.

"May I help you?" the receptionist asks when it's your turn.

"I'm a computer support specialist here on loan from the city. I'm supposed to meet with Maritza Quintana," you answer.

"Oh, I'm sorry you had to wait. She's in the administrative office on the sixth floor," the receptionist says. He points to the elevator.

On the sixth floor, Maritza comes out of her office and introduces herself. "Welcome to the Y. We're so glad the city sent you to help us. We're clearly not computer experts."

"I never realized how much the YMCA does," you answer.

Maritza laughs. "And you don't even know about the job training program, the learning center, and our daycare program. They're all computerized," she says.

"Which brings up the reason I'm here. What exactly do you want my help with?" you ask.

"Well," Maritza begins, "I talked to all our departments—from administration to the exercise club. I asked for information about their computer needs. Here's the list. It's quite varied. For example, the learning center staff needs information on computers and education choices. They want you to load some new **software**. The accounting office is wondering what's wrong with one **terminal**. There are several requests for you to assess **hardware** problems on other floors."

"Before I look over the wish list, I need to understand more about your computer use throughout the whole building," you tell her.

As you think about the work requests at the YMCA, you plan ahead. First you need to **understand the Y's computer system.** Then you can use the Y's resources to **prioritize the work requests.** You will use information to **follow instructions to install software.** You'll need to **listen to the computer users** to learn details about what they want. Finally, you will **locate a computer malfunction** for the clients.

SUMMARIZE THE TASKS

There are five tasks that you will accomplish in this lesson. They are in **bold** type above. Write the tasks on the correct lines below.

CATEGORY	TASK	ORDER	PAGE
Resources	_____	___	114
Information	_____	___	116
Systems	*understand a computer system*	*1*	118
Interpersonal	_____	___	121
Technology and Tools	_____		123

PLAN YOUR TIME

How can you plan your time to do all these tasks? Are there some tasks that need to be done first, before other tasks can be done? (*Hint:* Wouldn't you need to understand a computer system before you can prioritize the work requests?) In the ORDER column above, list the tasks in the order you will complete them.

THINK IT THROUGH

• What information will the Y need to give you so that you can do these tasks? • Who might be able to help?

▶ Now go to the task listed as 1 and continue the lesson.

Resources: Computer support specialists schedule time differently every day, because every day is different. When they schedule time, they list the work requests and prioritize them. Then they estimate the amount of time each task will take.

You should do the Systems task on page 118 before you begin this task.

PRIORITIZE WORK REQUESTS

Now that you understand the YMCA's use of computers, you need to evaluate the work requests and decide which to do first. Maritza's staff has asked you to

▶ solve some computer malfunctions
▶ install some software
▶ discuss computer choices for education with teachers

You can't prioritize the tasks until you have more information about them. You decide to question Maritza about the Y's computer needs.

For this task you ask questions to gain more information about computer problems. You will evaluate and prioritize the computer work requests.

Before you begin to ask questions, picture the task from beginning to end. • How will you find out what task is most important? • What information will you need? • Where will you get this information?

YOUR NOTES

You decide to question Maritza first, since she has arranged your visit and is fairly knowledgeable about computers. You ask her specific questions about each request. Complete the questions to ask Maritza below.

1. How urgent *is each problem?* _____

2. What kind of problems _____

3. Who has reported _____

4. Where are the _____

_____

Maritza tells you that the three hardware malfunctions are the most urgent problems:

Volunteer in fundraising drive reported his monitor is not working well. Fundraising is on 6th floor, in administration offices. Should you repair or replace?	Accountant reported problems with printer. Accounting is on 6th floor, in administration offices. Should you repair or replace?	Receptionist reported that **disk drive** isn't working. Receptionist is on first floor. Should you repair or replace?

Some teachers need you to install software and recommend new equipment.

Learning Center is on 4th floor; new math software is to be installed there.	Teachers work throughout building but can meet you in the Learning Center at 5:00 P.M. to discuss their needs.

Prioritize the five tasks listed above. List them in the order you'll work on them. Ask yourself, "What's most important?" "How can I save time while doing these tasks?"

1. _____

2. _____

3. _____

4. _____

5. _____

TASK RECAP

▶ Did you list all five tasks?

▶ Did you list the most urgent problems first?

Now that you have prioritized the work requests, think about it. • What would you do differently next time?

_____

_____

Information: Computer support specialists need information on new software and other computer equipment. This information is usually written in a manual or installed on a computer program. Computer support specialists must be able to follow directions and read through this information.

*You should do the Systems task on page 118 before you begin this task.

FOLLOW INSTRUCTIONS TO INSTALL SOFTWARE

It's time for you to install the math software in the Learning Center. You'll **load** the software on the IBM Novell networked machines. The software package has a notebook called *Installation* that contains loading instructions.

When installing software, follow these steps:

Step 1 Start one of the workstations.

Step 2 Insert a **floppy disk** in a disk drive.

Step 3 Type commands on the keyboard according to software installation directions.

Step 4 Test the installation to make sure it's correct.

For this task you will practice loading software on a computer. You will refer to the drawing on page 117 to do Steps 1–2 above. You'll need a computer or a typewriter keyboard to practice Step 3.

VISUALIZE THE WHOLE TASK

Before you begin to load the software, picture the task from beginning to end. • How will you find the meanings of some unfamiliar words? • How do you start a workstation? • Where is a disk drive?

YOUR NOTES
What information will you need before you can perform this task?
_____
_____
_____

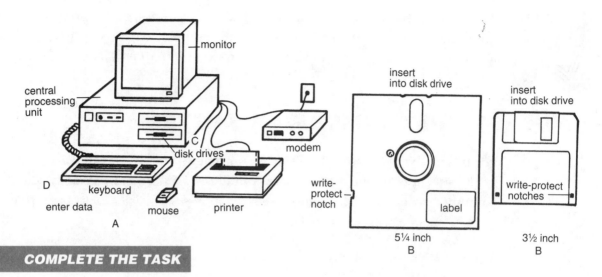

Study the workstation pictured above. Match the instructions below to the location (A–D).

1. Be seated at the workstation. _____   3. Put the disk in the disk drive. _____

2. Find the floppy disk. _____   4. Type commands. _____

5. Using a typewriter or computer keyboard, input the commands on the right. (*Your computer screen may not have the same commands as are given on the left below. Go ahead and type the commands on the right.*)

computer screen says: **you input:**

Login: *supervisor* (Enter/Return)

C:\>   *map* (Enter/Return)

Drive Y:= xxxxx/SYS:PUBLIC   place disk in drive A
                                              type *a:* (Enter/Return)

A>   *install y:\public\nmbp* (Enter/Return)

TASK RECAP

▶ Did you find what you needed on the drawing above?
▶ Did you input the commands carefully?

The software is now installed. • Did you use the steps you thought you'd use? • What would you change next time?

_____

_____

Systems: Both hardware (the computer itself) and software (the programs that run on computers) use systems. Within a computer network, each computer serves as a part of a system, and that system doesn't function well when one of its parts isn't working.

UNDERSTAND A COMPUTER SYSTEM

For this task you will study the YMCA computer system. You will learn what each part of the system does and how it relates to the rest of the system. Finally, you'll study a computer system on your own. *If there are any words you don't understand, find the meanings in the Glossary on pages 143–144.*

The sketch below tells you where, how many, and what kind of computers are at the Y. Look at the two drawings below.

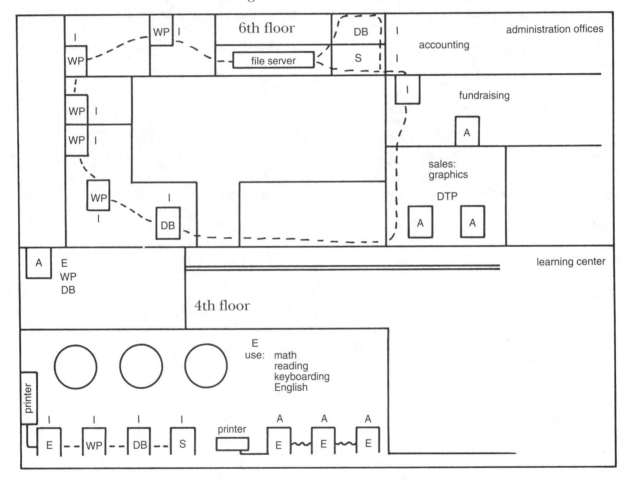

I = IBM compatible   A = Apple   ---- = **Networked** system

Software applications:

DB = **Data base**   S = **Spreadsheet**   WP = Word processing

E = Education   DTP = Desktop publishing

Study the diagram on page 118. Before you go study a computer system on your own, picture the task from beginning to end. • What will you be looking for? • What questions might you ask?

YOUR NOTES
List any questions you may have about the diagram on page 118.

Before you study a computer system on your own, answer these questions about the YMCA diagram on page 118.

1. What are computers used for at the YMCA? _____

   _____

2. What type of computers (hardware) does the Y have more of—IBM **compatibles** or Apple products? _____

3. Where are the networked (computers connected by cables) systems?_____

This diagram shows a typical computer workstation. Study it carefully.

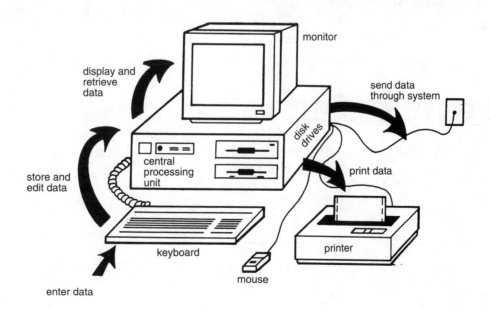

display and retrieve data

monitor

send data through system

store and edit data

disk drives

central processing unit

print data

keyboard

mouse

printer

enter data

Answer these questions about the workstation shown on page 119.

4. Why would computers be networked here? Why would these users need to communicate with each other?

   _____

5. What type of software applications does the Y have? _____

6. What does the CPU (Central Processing Unit) do? _____

7. What computer parts are used to enter data? _____

8. What two computer parts at this workstation display data? _____

9. Now complete the rest of your task. To research a computer network on your own, follow these steps:

Step 1   Decide where you'll go. Where have you seen computers in use? Offices? Libraries? Stores? Your community center or social service agency? Someone's workplace?

Step 2   Make an appointment with someone at this place who can discuss the computer system with you.

Step 3   Using the questions on page 119–120 as a guide, write sample questions about the hardware, software, network, and uses of computers at this place. Plan to ask about the problems and benefits of computer use as well.

Step 4   Summarize the information you've found. You could draw a diagram like the one on page 118. You could videotape the computer system. Or you could write and discuss what you've found.

TASK RECAP

▶ Did you write sample questions to cover all the suggested topics?
▶ Did you summarize your findings to show them to others?

REVIEW YOUR PLAN

Now that you've investigated a computer system, how did it go? • What did you learn? • What questions do you still have about it?

_____

_____

_____

Interpersonal: Computer support specialists need to be good listeners. Before they can help with technical problems, they must understand what their clients are saying. Computer support specialists spend time listening, analyzing, asking questions, and diagnosing problems.

You should do the Systems task on page 118 before you begin this task.

LISTEN TO COMPUTER USERS

For this task you will listen to what the computer users tell you. You need to listen carefully to find out exactly how you can help.

There are seven monitors in the Learning Center. With one glance you know that one problem the teachers have is old equipment. You approach the hardware to get a closer look at it.

"Hi, I'm Rosemary, a teacher here. You must be our computer expert from the mayor. I'll get the others," says an energetic young woman.

When the group is gathered, Rosemary begins, "Well, here is our computer lab. All of the equipment's been donated over the last three years, and we're using it as much as we know how. The Apples are hand-me-downs from the school district. They work well.

"Our IBMs are pretty slow, but the old software we have doesn't need much speed. New software requires faster hardware. The software programs we have to teach math, reading, GED subjects, and English as a second language aren't up-to-date anymore.

"We really want to keep up with new technology. We're thinking of applying for a grant to get newer, better computer equipment. We just don't know what we should ask for. Could you help us evaluate our needs and focus our grant proposal?"

VISUALIZE THE WHOLE TASK

Before you begin to sort through what you've heard, picture the task from beginning to end. • What does this task include? • What have the teachers told you here?

YOUR NOTES
What steps will you take now?
_____
_____
_____

Now evaluate what the teachers have told you on page 121. What needs are they describing? What information would a specialist be able to give them? Fill in the chart below with information you could give them.

Category	Teachers want	Information you could give
Hardware	*to keep up with new technology*	*technological advances made*
IBM hardware	*faster, more advanced to keep up with new software*	*new, faster IBM hardware available*
Apple hardware		
Networked workstations		
Stand-alone workstations		
Software		

TASK RECAP

▶ Did you find the teachers' needs in the narrative?
▶ Did you brainstorm on what information a specialist may have?

REVIEW YOUR PLAN

Now that you've evaluated the teachers' needs, what have you learned about listening to people? • How will you listen better next time?

_____

_____

_____

_____

Technology and Tools: Many computer support specialists enter this field because of their interest in technology. They need an ability to install hardware, load software, test systems, troubleshoot malfunctions, and train users in computer technology.

You should do the Systems task on page 118 before you begin this task.

LOCATE A COMPUTER MALFUNCTION

For this task you will check a computer monitor to see why it has malfunctioned. You will refer to a checklist and to diagrams. You will decide what is wrong with the monitor.

The fundraising volunteer reported that his monitor looks strange. You're checking it out. Here is your checklist of things to look for.

Visual Inspection	Check
Signs of overheating	☐
Discoloration (fried resistors)	☐
Bubbling or swelling (fried ICs, **capacitors**)	☐
Vaporization (blown fuses)	☐
Separation (blown fuses)	☐
Switches	☐
Power Lights	☐
Controls (Adjusted)	☐
Disconnections	
Separated plugs/sockets	☐
Loose wires	☐
Loose jumpers	☐
Cracked traces	☐
Misconnections	
Wrongly connected plugs/sockets	☐
Wrongly connected wires	☐
Wrongly configured jumpers	☐
Shorts between traces, wires, parts	☐
Mangling	
Parts bent over (potential shorts)	☐
Parts with twisted leads (potential shorts)	☐

Before you begin to check for the cause of the malfunction, picture the task from beginning to end. • What parts of the checklist will you use? • How will you know when you've found the problem?

YOUR NOTES
List the steps you'll take to check the monitor.
_____
_____

COMPLETE THE TASK

At this point, you inspect the monitor, following the checklist one item at a time. You've checked each item on the list below. Now put a check (✔) on the checklist on page 123 for each item below.

no overheating   no sign of blown fuses

the monitor on/off switch works   no disconnections

the power light works   monitor is connected to CPU

no discoloration on the outside   wires are connected correctly

brightness control works   no sign of shorts between traces, wires, parts

Maybe the problem is with the software. The colors aren't quite right; the purple background looks strange. Adjustments to both brightness and contrast work fine. You move through several color choice options within the software and they all change, but all of them look strange.

Now you realize that the problem is probably in the monitor, not the software. You decide to check for *mangling:* bent or twisted parts. The trouble might be in the cable connections.

Look at the cable connections on the back of the monitor.

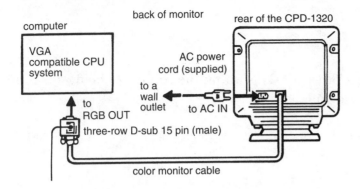

The color monitor cable connects to a socket with pins in it. When you pull the color monitor cable out from the CPU, the end looks like this:

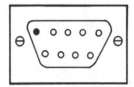

Your manual gives you this display:

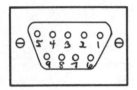

1 GROUND
2 GROUND (OR N/C)
3 RED
4 GREEN
5 BLUE
6 INTENSITY (OR N/C)
7 N/C
8 HORIZONTAL DRIVE
9 VERTICAL DRIVE

Compare the cable with the manual display. What is wrong with this monitor?

_____

_____

TASK RECAP

▶ Did you check off items on the manual checklist?
▶ Did you locate the problem?

REVIEW YOUR PLAN

Now that you've located a computer malfunction, what steps did you follow to do the task? • Were any steps unnecessary? • Why or why not?

_____

_____

USE WHAT YOU'VE LEARNED

You've been learning a variety of skills within the context of being a computer support specialist. Some of these skills are

- ▶ prioritizing requests
- ▶ following instructions
- ▶ understanding networks
- ▶ listening to others
- ▶ checking for problems with technology

1. Name two other jobs that might require these skills. How might these skills be put to use?

   Example: *a machinist needs to check for problems with technology*

   _____

   _____

2. Is there anywhere else you've used these skills? Where?

   Example: *I listen to others when I'm talking with my friends*

   _____

   _____

3. Now that you've completed the tasks in this lesson, can you think of two new tasks at work or at home that you might try? What are they?

   _____

   _____

   _____

   _____

ANSWER KEY

UNIT I

HEALTHCARE

ADJUST THE SCHEDULE: COMPLETE THE TASK

Pages 8–9

Answers will vary. Sylvie Hernandez and Jesse
Withers could both be rescheduled; neither has
emergency needs. They could be seen by Dr. Peltier
at 11:30 or by Dr. Michaels. A possible schedule is
shown below.

TIME	NAME	AGE	REASON FOR VISIT
8:30	Pete Wilson	48	mild chest pain two days ago
9:30	Helen Moore	37	foot surgery check back/out of cast ?
10:00	Benita Jordan	82	fatigue/cough and cold
10:30	"	"	
11:00	Luke Nguyen	2 mo.	cold/cough for two days; no temp
11:30 / 12:00 noon	either Sylvie Hernandez or Jesse Withers scheduled, depending on their preference. Peltier on hospital rounds.		

PRIORITIZE MEDICAL INFORMATION: COMPLETE THE TASK

Pages 10–12

1. pneumonia, rheumatoid arthritis, sight loss,
   hearing loss, weight gain
2. cold, cough, tired, sore ankle, stays in wheelchair
3.

RHEUMATOID ARTHRITIS	PNEUMONIA	HEART FAILURE
tired (fatigue)	cough won't go away	tired (fatigue)
sore ankle (joint pain)		rapid weight gain
		cough

4. Answers will vary, but should include the information from 3. A possible Physician Communication form is shown below.

PHYSICIAN COMMUNICATION FORM

Instructions for use: Address communications. Sign communication, cross out when received and complete. Flip blue Alert clip to indicate message to be read.

Date/Time	To:
yesterday's date	patient phoned complaining of chronic cough and cold, fatigue, pain in ankle, reduced mobility

---

PLAN EXAM PROCEDURE: COMPLETE THE TASK
Pages 13–14

1. Answers will vary.
2. Answers will vary. Possible answers include:
   2. push patient's wheelchair into exam room
   3. complete as much of exam as possible in the wheelchair or use another chair if possible
   4. c. bring scale into exam room so she doesn't have to move to the scale
   5. speak very clearly; look at patient when speaking to her so that she hears you well
   8. try to schedule tests today; it's difficult for patient to get to office
   10. arrange for help in getting patient from place to place in clinic; patient has trouble getting around in wheelchair

BUILD A TEAM: COMPLETE THE TASK
Pages 15–17

Answers will vary. Possible answers include:

1. use polite language; be understanding if a person can't help you; treat each person as your equal

"I know you've got a full day, but could you possibly help me with a patient between 10:00 and 10:30 A.M. tomorrow?"

2. ask as soon as you know what you'll need; give people time to think about it; ask for the most important things first
"Mrs. Jordan wants to visit accounting tomorrow morning around 11:00 A.M. Could you possibly prepare her records in advance so she won't have to wait?"

3. describe exactly what, when, and why you need help; give possible options
"Mrs. Jordan has some serious problems and we'd like to take care of all her needs tomorrow. She'll be in at 10:30. When I give you the blood sample, could you test it right away?"

4. "would you have time to . . ." "would it be possible for you to . . ." "Would you have time to help a patient tomorrow morning?"

5. Answers will vary.

UPDATE A MEDICAL RECORD: COMPLETE THE TASK

Pages 18–19

1. Answers will vary.
2. The medical record should look like the one below.

GROUP HEALTH HOSPITAL PHYSICIAN PROGRESS RECORD	
DATE OF ADMISSION	**TIME**
DATE & TIME	**NOTE** PROGRESS OF PATIENT, COMPLICATIONS, CONSULTATION, CHANGE IN DIAGNOSIS, CONDITION ON DISCHARGE AND INSTRUCTIONS TO PATIENT
yesterday's date	Patient phoned complaining of chronic cough and cold, fatigue, pain in ankle, reduced mobility
today's date	Vitals: T. 102.4 Pulse 85 Wt. 208 respiration 20 w/wheezing BP 160/95

USE WHAT YOU'VE LEARNED

Page 20

Answers will vary.

UNIT II

EDUCATION AND HUMAN SERVICES

MANAGE TODAY'S ACTIVITIES: COMPLETE THE TASK

Pages 26–27

Schedules will vary. Each of the daily activities should be covered. They should also be scheduled at appropriate times of day. A possible schedule is shown on page 130.

TIME	ACTIVITY	STAFFPERSON: you/David
10:00–10:30	indoor gym	David (you could be tending to Nick's scrapes)
10:30–11:00	snack	David (you could be planning arts/crafts project)
11:00–12:00	arts/crafts	you and David
12:00–1:00	lunch and clean up	you and David
1:00–1:30	storytime	David (you could be working out the Tina/Nick incident)
1:30–2:30	naptime	You (David could be working on games for outside play)
2:30–3:00	snack	You (David could be picking songs for music)
3:00–4:00	outdoor play	you and David
4:00–4:30	music	you
4:30–5:30	free play	you and David
5:30–6:00	final cleanup	you and David

COMMUNICATE INFORMATION: COMPLETE THE TASK
Pages 28–29
Answers will vary. Your conversation outline should be completed, and you should have tried to solve the problem in a positive way.

EVALUATE THE CENTER'S POLICY: COMPLETE THE TASK
Pages 30–31
1. Tina tripped Nick.
2. Answers will vary.
3. Answers will vary.
4. Marilyn, the other staff, the parents
5. Marilyn
6. Answers will vary. Your rewritten policy should say that a child who emotionally teases or taunts another child will be disciplined.

CREATE A MEETING AGENDA: COMPLETE THE TASK

Pages 32–33

Answers will vary. Your meeting agenda should follow a logical order. A possible agenda is shown below.

MEETING AGENDA	what to cover	who is responsible
1. Introductions	who everyone is	everyone introduces self
2. Reason for meeting	why meeting is needed	you
3. Goals	what you want to do	you
4. Agenda	order of meeting	you
5. Time limit	how long you will meet	you/parents
6. Review	what happened with the children	You
7. Varied viewpoints	how everyone feels	you/parents
8. Consensus	everyone agrees	you/parents
9. Decision making	what will happen	you/parents
10. Assignments made	what everyone will do	you/parents
11. Summary	what decisions were made	you
12. Closing	thanks and goodbyes	you

SELECT TECHNOLOGY FOR TINA: COMPLETE THE TASK

Pages 34–35

Answers will vary. You should have chosen toys and technology that appeal to Tina's building and electronic skills and that she may teach or share with the other children.

USE WHAT YOU'VE LEARNED

Page 36

Answers will vary.

MANUFACTURING AND MECHANICAL

MANAGE TIME TO MEET PRINTING DEADLINES: COMPLETE THE TASK

Pages 40–41

Answers will vary. You should have
- replaced your 8:00 A.M. to 10:00 A.M. job with something else
- rescheduled the Homeland order after 10:00 A.M. and given it a 2-hour time slot
- scheduled each job that was originally listed
- allowed time for both preparation (45 minutes/job) and printing (1 hour/3,000 copies)

A possible schedule is shown below.

PRINTING SCHEDULES

Henry's schedule		Your schedule	
8:00 A.M.	RR + 2,000	8:00 A.M.	NP + 6,000
9:00 A.M.		9:00 A.M.	
10:00 A.M.	RR + 3,000	10:00 A.M.	
11:00 A.M.		11:00 A.M.	
12:00 P.M.	Lunch	12:00 P.M.	
1:00 P.M.	RR + 2,000	1:00 P.M.	Lunch
2:00 P.M.		2:00 P.M.	RR + 3,000
3:00 P.M.	3:30 NP + 1,500	3:00 P.M.	
4:00 P.M.		4:00 P.M.	RR + 1,000
5:00 P.M.		5:00 P.M.	

PREPARE JOB PRINTING INFORMATION: COMPLETE THE TASK

Pages 42–43

1. 8½ × 11; 24 lb. 175
2. black, PMS 178
3. TD
4. No
5. 1250
6. change Carl to Carol
7. yes
8. a new plate will have to be made
9. Archie Larson

LEARN PRINT SHOP ORGANIZATIONAL STRUCTURE: COMPLETE THE TASK

Pages 44–45

Offset Press Operator Duty?	Task	Order in Process
	billing the customer	18
X	inking rollers	10
	shipping	17
X	adjusting the ink rollers	12
	setting the type	4
	developing film	5
X	checking a sample against the proof	11
	estimating document cost	2
	making the plate	6
X	attaching plate to cylinder	9
	binding	14
	writing a packing list	15
X	checking the water level	8
	taking the customer order	1
	completing job order form	3
	packing the printed documents	16
X	checking the paper stock	7
X	printing documents	13

ASK QUESTIONS ABOUT A JOB: COMPLETE THE TASK

Pages 46–47

Answers will vary.

MAKE QUALITY CONTROL ADJUSTMENTS TO A PRESS: COMPLETE THE TASK

Pages 48–49

1. ink isn't coming evenly through the plate onto the paper
2. the ink fountain keys
3. you should have marked fountain keys

USE WHAT YOU'VE LEARNED

Page 50

Answers will vary.

COLLECT APPROPRIATE RESOURCES: COMPLETE THE TASK

Pages 54–56

Answers will vary. Possible answers include

1.a. Florida airline flight info   b. *OAG North American Edition*

Hawaii airline flight info   *OAG North American Edition*

Hotel descriptions:
Disney World   *Hotel and Travel Index*
OAG Hotel and Motel Redbook

Hotel descriptions: Hawaii   *OHRG Worldwide Edition*
OAG Hotel and Motel Redbook

2.a. cost of plane tickets   b. I could call the airline
space availability at hotel   I could call the hotel
brochures on the hotel   look in office files or request from hotel

car rental rates and info   car rental brochures phoning rental companies

sight-seeing information   look in office files or call Chambers of Commerce

3.–7. Answers will vary depending on the choices made by the person you interviewed.

PRESENT VACATION INFORMATION: COMPLETE THE TASK

Pages 57–59

Category	Royal Hawaiian	Ambassador Hotel of Waikiki	Pagoda Hotel
cost (double room)	$210 – $315	$80 – 165	$90 – 105
features	good service, luxury redecorated rooms, views of ocean	near Waikiki, comfortable rooms, kitchens, private lanai	remodeled rooms, refrigerators or kitchenettes
services	food, shopping, parking	cafe, parking, drinks	restaurant, on bus line
recreation	pool, golf, historic site	pool	pool, shopping
location	Honolulu, on ocean	Honolulu	Honolulu

UNDERSTAND AGENCY SERVICES AND BILLING: COMPLETE THE TASK
Pages 60–61

1. $360 × .12 (12%) = $43.20
2. $89.54 × .08 (8%) = $7.16
3. $43.20 and $7.16
4. Your bill should look like this:

Billing Information	Transportation Air/Ground	Accommodations Hotel/Motel	Meals B/L/D	Activity Car Rental
Cost	$823	$360		$89.54
% commission	9%	12%		8%
Amount billed	$74.07	$43.20		$7.16
Total	$74.07	$43.20		$7.16

INTERVIEW A CUSTOMER: COMPLETE THE TASK
Pages 62–63

Answers will vary.

COMPLETE A CONFIRMATION SHEET: COMPLETE THE TASK
Pages 64–65

Answers will vary.

USE WHAT YOU'VE LEARNED
Page 66

Answers will vary.

UNIT III

FINANCIAL SERVICES

SERVE CUSTOMERS WITH AVAILABLE STAFF: COMPLETE THE TASK
Pages 72–73

1. Answers will vary. A possible diagram is below:

Window 1	Window 2	Window 3
You	*Summer*	*Chris*
solve account problems	money orders	deposits
provide account information	deposits	withdrawals
	check cashing	
	withdrawals	

2. You could make signs to direct customers to specific lines; you could ask the assistant manager to direct them.

COMPLETE A BANK TRANSACTION: COMPLETE THE TASK

Pages 74–75

1. Answers will vary.
2. Step 1 "May I see your identification, please?"
   Step 2 yes
   Step 3 account number: 0080420
               deposit amount: $1,019.23

FILL OUT AN EYEWITNESS REPORT: COMPLETE THE TASK

Pages 76–77

Answers will vary. Possible answers include:

1. wearing black helmet, black leather jacket and pants
2. black Honda with silver trim
3. 2 bags on seat behind man; reflector on side of motorcycle
4. Your report could look something like this:

IDENTIFICATION REPORT

Witness name: *(your name)*   Date: *(today's date)*

Type of incident: *bank robbery*   Location: Midtown Mutual Savings Bank

Description of incident:
Bank teller Javier Gomez was robbed shortly before lunchtime by a white man wearing a black leather jacket and pants. The robber claimed to know where Javier's wife works and threatened to hurt Javier's wife if he didn't cooperate. The robber sped away on a black Honda motorcycle with silver trim and a reflector on the side. Two bags were on the seat behind the man.

Witness signature: *(your signature)*   Officer signature:

SUPPORT THE MEMBERS OF YOUR TEAM: COMPLETE THE TASK

Pages 78–79

Answers will vary. Possible answers include:

1. "It's been a hard day. Are you sure you're OK?"
2. "I was very impressed with how you handled the customers today. In fact, when I heard how you answered their questions, I began using the same answers you did."
3. "Javier did exactly what he should have done. He really kept his head during the robbery."
4. "Thanks for picking up the extra work today. I don't know what we'd have done without you."
5. Conversations will vary.

BALANCE A CASH DRAWER: COMPLETE THE TASK

Pages 80–81

1. withdrew $1,400.00 cash, leaving a balance of $6,600.00
2. c

Your completed balance sheet should look like this:

Balance Sheet							
Time	Cash Bal	A#	With/A	Ty	Dep/A	Ty	Cash Bal
9:30 AM	8000.00						8000.00
9:31	8000.00	0077412			1846.22	ch	8000.00
9:40	8000.00	0084361	1400.00	c			6600.00
9:53	6600.00	0141233	300.00	c	470.37	ch	6300.00
9:59	6300.00	1004217			789.32	ch	6300.00
10:04	6300.00	0378400	48.95	ch	502.02	c	6802.02
10:09	6802.02	0062417			2317.62	ch	6802.02
10:11	6802.02	0499828			1730.00	c	8532.02
10:29	8532.02	1783692	150.00	c	300.00	ch	8382.02
10:35	8382.02	0023476			4572.36	ch	8382.02
10:39	8382.02	9923476	350.00	c			8032.02
10:49	8032.02	8519540	2000.00	c			6032.02
11:16	6032.02	5549012	350.98	c	5076.39	ch	5681.04
11:22	5681.04	0012874	1357.00	c	17456.00	ch	4324.04
11:28	4324.04	0499662	450.00	c	10598.32	ch	3874.04
11:35	3874.04	9098123			6500.00	c	10374.04
11:50	10374.04	7659901	125.75	c	500.00	ch	10248.29
11:58	10248.29	4466291	250.00	c	950.00	ch	9998.29
12:03 PM	ROBBERY						

3. $9,998.29

USE WHAT YOU'VE LEARNED
Page 82
Answers will vary.

HOSPITALITY SERVICES

PREPARE A SCHEDULE: COMPLETE THE TASK

Pages 86–87

A possible schedule is shown below.

HEAD HOUSEKEEPING SCHEDULE   DATE: (*today's date*)

Cleaning time:

30 minutes/vacated room (v)

15 minutes/occupied room (o)

Staff	Caroline	Tanya	Tuyet	Tatiana	Head Housekeeper
8:30 A.M.		501	807(o), 812(o)	Train with Head	217
9:00		502(o), 505, 511(o)	827, 831	Housekeeper	222, 228
10:00		520, 522, 548(o)	840(o), 842, 849	↓	230, 235, 237(o)
11:15	break	break	break	break	break
11:30		603, 610(o), 612(o)	903, 909	239, 240	inspect 4 rooms
12:30 P.M.	lunch	lunch	lunch	lunch	lunch
1:30		618, 625	917(o), 920, 922(o)	Work with Tuyet	308, 321
2:30		628(o), 630, 641	928, 933, 940(o)	↓	inspect 4 rooms
3:45	break	break	break	break	break
4:00		700(o), 703, 712(o)	1001, 1019	336(o), 342	select new vacuum cleaner
5:00		728(o), 734(o)	1027(o), 1039(o)	346	train Tatiana
5:30		411	426	403	

TRAIN A NEW HOUSEKEEPER: COMPLETE THE TASK

Pages 88–89

Answers will vary.

INSPECT A CLEANED BATHROOM: COMPLETE THE TASK

Pages 90–91

Answers will vary. However, you should have rejected the housekeeper's work.

SUPERVISE A CULTURALLY DIVERSE STAFF: COMPLETE THE TASK

Pages 92–93

Answers will vary.

SELECT A NEW VACUUM CLEANER: COMPLETE THE TASK

Pages 94–95

1. Your chart should look like this:

Features	Riccar Model 2200	Panasonic MC-6217
weight/portability	15 lbs.	15 lbs.
adjust to different carpet heights?	yes	yes
various handle positions	yes; 3 positions	yes; 3 positions
dust capacity	9 quarts	10 quarts
cord length and release	40 foot grounded cord	33 foot cord
metal brushes	12" steel 4 replaceable brushes	14" metal all-brush agitator
filter system	triple clean air filtration	triple filter system
edge cleaning	yes	yes
motor size	7.8 amp	7.0 amp
optional tools	6 piece - 8 piece	no
headlight	yes	yes
other		

2. Answers will vary.
3. Answers will vary.

USE WHAT YOU'VE LEARNED
Page 96

Answers will vary.

COMMUNICATION AND SALES
SCHEDULE TIME: COMPLETE THE TASK
Pages 100–101

Answers will vary. Your chart should include each task in the lesson, and you should have estimated when you'd finish and how much time you'd need.

SHARE INFORMATION WITH A CUSTOMER: COMPLETE THE TASK
Pages 102–103

1. they don't like cooking outside; the food takes too long to cook; the barbecue grill is too big; it's not useful to them
2. they want to stay inside; they want to cook more quickly; they need something smaller
3. Answers will vary. Possible answers include:

Appliance	Why?	Why not?
smaller barbecue grill		they don't like to barbecue
toaster oven	it's inside and can cook small items quickly	
table top gas grill	it's small and lights more quickly and easily	
microwave oven	it's inside; food cooks quickly; it's not too large	

4. Whichever product you chose, you should have described it carefully and completely to your partner.

UNDERSTAND A RETURN/EXCHANGE POLICY: COMPLETE THE TASK
Pages 104–105
Your return/exchange form should look like this:

2959524	SHIPPING CODE	DIVISION	SALES NO.	SALES DATE	SELLING STORE NO. 406

SC/CLC 0	CASH 1	COD 2	DC 3	MCA 5	SCRCP 6	EP/MCP 7			DELAY BILL DATE MONTH / DAY / CODE	DEF	PMT MONTH

ACCOUNT NUMBER	9833 391 266 994	APPROVAL

NAME (PRINT) **Clyde and Shirley Mueller**

ADDRESS **P.O. Box 72**

CITY Tunica	STATE MS	ZIP CODE 38676	PHONE 555-0437

DELIVERY DATE ▸	MO.	DAY	ROUTE NO. ▸		TYPE DEL. ▸	HANDLING CODE ▸	AREA CODE

SHIP FROM
☐ STORE STOCK ☐ STORE WHSE.
☐ C.M.D.C. ☐ DIST. CTR.

REASON FOR RETURN **gift, didn't like**

QTY.	STOCK NO/ MISC ACCT	DESCRIPTION	REGULAR PRICE	SELLING REDUCTION	SELLING PRICE
1	204498	Barbecue Grill	189.95	9.96	179.99
			SALES TAX 7.9% ▸		14.22
	Clyde Mueller		DEPOSIT ▸		
	PURCHASED BY		BALANCE ▸		194.21

COMMUNICATE WITH A CUSTOMER: COMPLETE THE TASK
Pages 106–107
Answers will vary. Possible answers include:

2. "How can someone not like a barbecue grill, especially as a gift?"
   This statement criticizes the customers for not liking the gift.
3. "I guess your kids got it wrong, huh?"
   This statement implies that the children did not pick a good gift.
4. "Don't like to barbecue? Impossible. Everyone likes it. It's the best way to cook."
   This statement implies that the Muellers are "abnormal" and have poor taste in food.
5. "So what do you want to do about it? Return? Exchange? I have lots of forms to fill out and my head hurts."
   This statement is rude. It makes the customers feel as if they're intruding on the worker's time. It also is not helpful. Few customers would want to buy something else if spoken to like this.
6. Conversations will vary.

COMPLETE A SALES TRANSACTION:
COMPLETE THE TASK
Pages 108–109
Answers will vary.

USE WHAT YOU'VE LEARNED
Page 110
Answers will vary.

OFFICE SERVICES
PRIORITIZE WORK REQUESTS: COMPLETE
THE TASK
Pages 114–115
Answers will vary. However, you should probably do the three urgent tasks first (the monitor, printer, and disk drive). This makes sense; you can't talk to the teachers until 5:00 P.M. To save time, you could choose to work floor-by-floor: the first, the sixth, then the fourth.

FOLLOW INSTRUCTIONS TO INSTALL
SOFTWARE: COMPLETE THE TASK
Pages 116–117
1. A
2. B
3. C
4. D
5. You should have typed the exact information listed under *you input*.

UNDERSTAND A COMPUTER SYSTEM:
COMPLETE THE TASK
Pages 118–120
1. education, accounting, fundraising, membership, sales, administration
2. more IBM than Apples
3. administration, accounting, fundraising, sales/graphics, learning center
4. Answers will vary, but may include: Administrators might need other staff to help write a memo or report. They might send notes and documents to each other through the network. Accounting needs to communicate with the areas where money is handled (front desk, fundraising). Sales/graphics needs information from all departments to create its brochures. Learning Center needs software programs to be available to more than one student at a time.
5. word processing; data bases and spreadsheets; desktop publishing; math, keyboarding, reading, English
6. stores and edits data
7. keyboard and mouse
8. monitor and printer
9. Your findings on computer systems will vary.

LISTEN TO COMPUTER USERS: COMPLETE
THE TASK
Pages 121–122
Your chart should look something like this:

Category	Teachers want	Information you could give
Hardware	*to keep up with new technology*	*technological advances made*
IBM hardware	*faster, more advanced to keep up with new software*	*new, faster IBM hardware available*
Apple hardware	more advanced to keep up with new software	new Apple hardware available
Networked workstations	newer, better computer equipment	how much networks might cost. What networks can and can't do
Stand-alone workstations	newer, better computer equipment	how much stand-alones might cost. what they can and can't do
Software	newer educational software that may require advanced hardware	new software available; software compatibility with hardware

LOCATE A COMPUTER MALFUNCTION: COMPLETE THE TASK
Pages 123–125

1. The problem with the monitor is in the color monitor cable. The blue #5 pin has broken off from the CPU and is embedded in the cable. This causes the color mixtures to be off when software is run.

USE WHAT YOU'VE LEARNED
Page 126
Answers will vary.

GLOSSARY

accommodates: adjusts for differences

account: a record of money paid out and money received

administrative: management responsibilities

agenda: a list of items of business to be considered at a meeting

appropriate: especially suitable or fitting

capacitors: devices for storing electric charges

central processing unit (CPU): the microprocessor in a computer that contains thousands of electronic switches to execute program instructions and to process data

certificate of deposit (CD): a type of savings account that earns a higher rate of interest but requires a minimum deposit, which must be left in the account for a fixed period of time or a penalty must be paid for early withdrawal

compatibles: computer systems that are similar enough to be used in conjunction with one another

courier: messenger service

data base: a collection of information that is organized especially to be used by a computer

data tracking: making sure figures and account information are up-to-date, or current

deposit slip: a form provided by a bank that is filled out to show how much money is being deposited, or put into, an account

disk drive: the mechanism that reads the magnetic medium that carries the information for a computer to use

flexible: capable of responding to new situations

floppy disk: a small flexible disk with a magnetic coating on which data for a computer can be stored

hardware: the equipment that makes up a computer system, including such items as the keyboard, mouse, disk drives, and monitor

input: to enter data into a computer

investment: the outlay of money for profit or purchase

load: install, or set up for use

malfunction: a failure to operate properly

modem: a device that enables a computer to transmit information over a telephone line

monitor: *(v)* watch, observe, or check; *(n)* a video screen used for display of computer information

mouse: a hand-held device that allows a person to point to and access information on a computer screen

networked: a series of computers connected by cables so that information can be shared among them

offset lithographic press: a large machine that prints from a flat surface, like a metal plate, that has been prepared in such a way that only the areas meant to print will take ink

personnel: the department that handles the hiring and firing of employees, and explaining company benefits and policies

Physician Progress Record: the form a doctor fills out about a patient's condition, treatment, response, and discharge instructions

policies: rules, plans, or courses of action

prioritize: put in order of importance

procedure: manner or method in which a business or an action is carried on

representative: a person who stands in or acts for another, especially through delegated authority

securities: stock certificates or bonds

software: the set of instructions, including the program, operating systems, device drivers, and applications, that makes a computer perform tasks

specification sheet: a detailed list of items or features that are part of a product

spreadsheet: a form generated on a computer that has several columns of numbers

terminal: a device that is connected to a communication network and is used to enter, receive, and display information

transaction: an act of communication between people in a business or a social situation

unpredictable: not able to tell in advance what might happen

verification: the act of proving something to be true, correct, or accurate

warranties: promises made by companies that their products meet a certain standard of quality

withdrawals: removing money from bank accounts

DOCTOR'S SCHEDULE

TIME	NAME	AGE	REASON FOR VISIT
8:30 A.M.			
9:30			
10:00			
10:30			
11:00			
11:30			
12:00 noon			

GROUP HEALTH HOSPITAL
PHYSICIAN PROGRESS RECORD

DATE OF ADMISSION		TIME

DATE & TIME	NOTE PROGRESS OF PATIENT, COMPLICATIONS, CONSULTATION, CHANGE IN DIAGNOSIS, CONDITION ON DISCHARGE AND INSTRUCTIONS TO PATIENT

MEDICAL INFORMATION

Heart Failure

OBSERVATIONS

Fatigue
Effort intolerance
Anorexia
Nausea and vomiting
Tachypnea
Dyspnea
Orthopnea
Tachycardia
Cyanosis
Restlessness
Cough
Rales, rhonchi
Rapid weight gain
Edema—firm, pitting, dependent
Ascites
Abdominal pain
Abdominal distention
Increased venous pressure
Distended neck veins
Diaphoresis
Hypokalemia
Drug toxicity

Rheumatoid Arthritis

OBSERVATIONS

Fatigue
Malaise
Weight loss
Joint pain and stiffness
Joint inflammation
    Redness
    Swelling
    Tenderness
    Warmth
Elevated temperature (low grade)
Muscular
    Weakness
    Spasms
    Atrophy
Subcutaneous nodules over bony
prominences—hands, elbows, knees
Behavioral changes
    Depression
    Anxiety
Renal calculi
Gastrointestinal bleeding

Pneumonia

OBSERVATIONS

Difficult and painful respirations
    Pleuritic pain
    Shortness of breath and grunting
    Tachypnea
    Diminished progressing to absent
    breath sounds
    Rales, rhonchi
    Unequal chest movements
Chills and fever (102° to 106°F)—delirium
Anorexia
Malaise
Abdominal distention

Productive, tenacious cough
    Incessant, painful
    Copious amounts of green-yellow
    sputum progressing to pink or rusty
Cyanosis
    Circumoral
    Nailbeds
Tachycardia
Pleural effusion
Lung abscess
Bacteremia

JOB SHEET

CUSTOMER NAME		1ST PROOF DATE		☐ Promised	ACCOUNT NO.
H O M E L A N D R E A L T Y					7 3 7 7 2 0

ADDRESS		2ND PROOF DATE		☐ Promised	JOB NO.
3 8 6 3 C H U R C H S T					0 2 7 8 1 2 0 9

CITY	ZIP	PRINT DATE	BINDERY DATE	DATE RECEIVED
C H A T T A N O O G A	3 7 4 0 9			

CONTACT PERSON	TELEPHONE	DELIVERY DATE		☐ Promised	CUSTOMER ORDER NO.
A R C H I E L A R S O N	4 8 6 - 8 2 7 7				7 8 1 1 3 1 4 5

DESCRIPTION
R E R U N   O F   L E T T E R H E A D

INSTRUCTIONS
Please change Carl to Carol; new president

PRE-PRESS	PRESS	PAPER	BILLING
☐ Galleys	☑ 1250	$8\frac{1}{2} \times 11$ 24 lb. 175	
☐ Comp/Paste	☐ 1250W		
☐ Prints	☐ Chief		Cutting
☐ Negatives	☐ TCS	SUPPLIER ORDER TAKER *TD* DATE ORDERED INK *Black*	TOTAL
☐ Other: _____	☐ Heidelberg		
	☐ Other _____	COMMENTS *Pms 178*	

PLATES		BILLING
PLATES	BURNS	
PLATES IN FILE 1		
		TOTAL

PRESS	
SIDES 1	UP
☐ Work & Turn ☐ Work & Tumble	
WASH-UPS 1	UNITS
PRESS TIME 3000	
COUNT PRESS OPERATOR DATE	
☐ Score	UNITS
☐ Perf	
☐ Die Cut ☐ Blind Emboss	
☐ Number START NO. END NO.	
COUNT PRESS OPERATOR DATE	
☐ Outside	TOTAL

BINDERY		
☐ Trim	FINISH SIZE	UNITS
☐ Pad	UP PADDED EDGE	UNITS
SHEETS / PAD	NO. OF PADS ☐ NCR ☐ Red Pad	
☐ Fold		UNITS
☐ Punch	NO. OF HOLES HOLE SIZE	

BINDERY (Cont.)			
☐ Corner Round	NO. OF CORNERS	LOCATION	UNITS
☐ Machine Gather	PARTS	SETS	
☐ Hand Gather	PARTS	SETS	
☐ Stitch	STICHES / PIECE	PIECES	
☐ Staple	STAPLES / PIECE	PIECES	TOTAL
☐ GBC ☐ Vello ☐ Heat	NO. OF BOOKS	THICKNESS	
☐ Other			
☐ Outside			TOTAL

PACKING & SHIPPING			
☑ Packing List ☑ Reorder Envelope			
NO. PER PACK 500		NO. OF PACKS 6	
☐ UPS	DATE	INITIALS	COMMENTS
☐ Cab			
☐ Other			
☑ Fine Delivery ☐ Customer Pickup			
SPECIAL DELIVERY INSTRUCTIONS			TOTAL

Total Price	
Sales Tax	
Subtotal	
Postage	
Total Billing	

FINE PRINTING SHOP STRUCTURE

Customer order taken by shop manager

↓

Cost estimate prepared by shop manager

↓

Typesetting pasteup

↓

Typesetter enters text on computer, coding typeface and type size. The text is printed onto film or paper.

Camera

↓

Negatives of the order are created and "stripped" to reveal light in the desired places.

Plate production

↓

Plate is coated with light-sensitive coating. Light is shown through negative film to expose the plate. Plate is developed so that the text and picture form.

Printing

↓

The plate is put on the press, inked appropriately, and the press runs, producing the final print.

Binding/Folding/Finishing

↓

The printed product is folded or bound with cording to a cover according to customer specifications.

Receipt and packing slip created

↓

Materials packed

↓

Order delivered to customer

↓

Customer billed for order

OFFSET PRESS OPERATOR

To print a product on the press, follow these steps:

Step 1 When you begin a job, you start at the job order. The order form should tell you all you need to run the order.

Step 2 Check your paper stock to make sure it's dry and not flawed.

Step 3 Mix inks to match the ink requested on the order.

Step 4 Check that your water is at an appropriate level to both cool the press and dampen the rollers.

Step 5 Attach the plate to the cylinders.

Step 6 Apply ink and run a sample document. Check the sample against the proof. Adjust the press, ink, pressure, and/or water until the samples are correct.

Step 7 While the press is running the order, monitor the final document quality and adjust the press as needed.

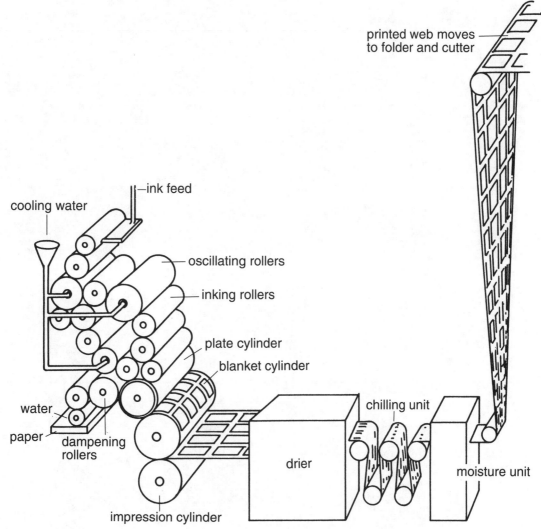

SCRIPT—OFFSET PRESS OPERATOR

[Scene: lunchtime; you and Leon are sitting at the outside picnic table]

You: "Ah, some sunshine. A nice change from the shop."

Leon: "If I stay inside, I not only work during lunch, I start molding to my chair."

You: "Well, I thought about getting to know the shop better, and decided to start with you. How long have you worked in printing?"

Leon: "Since I graduated from high school about 18 years ago. I first started packing and delivering orders. I worked my way into operating presses. Of course, everything in the printing business has changed since then. I've taken classes to keep up."

You: "Are the classes about running the shop?"

Leon: "It depends on what I need. Sometimes they're about new technologies. Sometimes they're about managing the shop, like how to create employee teams or new marketing strategies. Everything about business changes. I'm even planning training programs with people."

You: "Like the one I just finished?"

Leon: "Exactly. Printers are worried that people aren't finding out about printing careers, and we need more trained employees."

You: "So, my training as an offset press operator is done, but it's clear my print shop training isn't. What should I do next?"

Leon: "Well, talking to me is a good start. Is there anything else you want to know about my job? Or, is there someone you work closely with that you need to talk with?"

You: "Well, I'm really curious about how you take an order—how you store so much information in your brain. Also, I'd like to know more about scheduling in the shop. I've always been curious about typesetting and how it works. Maybe Barbara wouldn't mind if I watched her working for a while."

ink rollers

plate
cylinder

computer
control box

blanket
cylinder

window
(paper
 exit)

ink
fountain

fountain keys
1–27

paper
exit

Homeland
 order

(ink too dark)

AIR TRANSPORTATION INFORMATION

Airline Codes:

AA American Airlines
UA United Airlines
CO Continental Airlines
DL Delta Airlines
TW Trans World Airlines

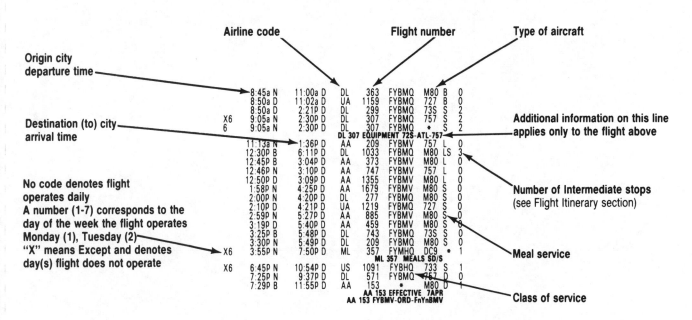

Origin city departure time

Airline code

Flight number

Type of aircraft

Destination (to) city arrival time

Additional information on this line applies only to the flight above

No code denotes flight operates daily
A number (1-7) corresponds to the day of the week the flight operates
Monday (1), Tuesday (2)
"X" means Except and denotes day(s) flight does not operate

Number of Intermediate stops (see Flight Itinerary section)

Meal service

Class of service

```
              8:45a N   11:00a D   DL    363   FYBMQ   M80  B  0
              8:50a D   11:02a D   UA   1159   FYBMQ   727  B  0
              8:50a D    2:21P D   DL    299   FYBMQ   73S  S  2
         X6   9:05a N    2:30P D   DL    307   FYBMQ   757  S  2
         6    9:05a N    2:30P N   DL    307   FYBMQ    *   S  2
                     DL 307 EQUIPMENT 72S-ATL-757
             11:13a N    1:36P D   AA    209   FYBMV   757  L  0
             12:30P B    6:11P D   DL   1033   FYBMQ   M80 LS  3
             12:45P B    3:04P D   AA    373   FYBMV   M80  L  0
             12:46P N    3:10P D   AA    747   FYBMV   757  L  0
             12:50P D    3:09P D   AA   1355   FYBMV   M80  L  0
              1:58P N    4:25P D   AA   1679   FYBMV   M80  S  0
              2:00P N    4:20P D   DL    277   FYBMQ   M80  S  0
              2:10P D    4:21P D   UA   1219   FYBMV   727  S  0
              2:59P N    5:27P D   AA    885   FYBMV   M80  S  0
              3:19P D    5:40P D   AA    459   FYBMV   M80  S  0
              3:25P B    5:48P D   DL    743   FYBMQ   73S  S  0
              3:30P N    5:49P D   DL    209   FYBMQ   M80  S  0
         X6   3:55P N    7:50P D   ML    357   FYMHQ   DC9  *  1
                     ML 357  MEALS SD/S
         X6   6:45P N   10:54P D   US   1091   FYBHQ   733  S  1
              7:25P N    9:37P D   DL    571   FYBMQ   757  D  0
              7:29P B   11:55P D   AA    153    *      M80  D  1
                     AA 153 EFFECTIVE 7APR
                  AA 153 FYBMV-ORD-FnYnBMV
```

Frequency Codes

1 — Monday
2 — Tuesday
3 — Wednesday
4 — Thursday
5 — Friday
6 — Saturday
7 — Sunday
X — Except

"SPEC" in the frequency column indicates the flight will operate on the dates specified on the following line.

Food Service

B Breakfast
D Dinner
F Food-available for purchase
L Lunch
S Snack

Fare/Class of Service Hierarchy

R Supersonic Aircraft
P First Class Premium
F First Class
A First Class Discounted
J Business Class Premium
C Business Class
D Business Class Discounted
S Economy/Coach
W Economy/Coach Premium
Fn Night Coach in First Class Compartment
Y Economy/Coach
Cn Night Business Coach
Yn Night Economy/Coach
B Economy/Coach Discounted
H Economy/Coach Discounted
Q Economy/Coach Discounted
M Economy/Coach Discounted
T Economy/Coach Discounted
K Economy/Coach Discounted
L Economy/Coach Discounted
V Economy/Coach Discounted
Bn Night Economy/Coach Discounted
Qn Night Economy/Coach Discounted
Kn Night Economy/Coach Discounted
Vn Night Economy/Coach Discounted
U Shuttle Service (No Reservation Needed - Seat Guaranteed)
E Shuttle Service (No Reservation Allowed)

To Orlando from Denver:

```
To ORLANDO, FLORIDA      EDT ORL

H-ORL (HERNDON)
O-MCO (ORLANDO INTERNATIONAL)

▲DENVER, COLORADO (D-DEN)      1548 Mi  MDT DEN
    9:35a D    4:40P O   NW    802   FYBMH   72S  S  1
   10:21a D    4:05P O   UA    835   FYBMQ   733  L  0
   10:21a D    4:12P O   CO   1566   FAYQH   M80  L  0
    3:27P D    9:04P O   UA    382   FYBMQ   757  D  0
                   EX AUG26
    6:16P D   12:14a O   CO    528   FAYQH   733  D  0
                   CONNECTIONS
    5:54a D    8:46a DFW AA   1844   FYBMV   M80  S  0
    9:25a DFW 12:56P O  AA   2032   FYBMV   M80  L  0
    6:05a D   11:19a IAD UA    264   FYBMQ   733  B  0
   12:02P IAD  2:04P O   UA    538   FYBMQ   72S  L/S 0
    6:15a D    9:02a DFW DL   1422   FYBMH   M80  B  0
    9:45a DFW  1:20P O   DL    778   FYBMH   757  B  0
X7  6:56a D   10:02a STL TW    436   FYBQV   M80  B  0
   10:56a STL  2:17P O   TW    498   FCYBQ   L10  L  0
7   6:56a D   10:02a STL TW    436   FYBQV   M80  B  0
   11:48a STL  3:06P O   TW    498   FCYBQ   L10  L  0
    7:40a D   12:25P ATL DL    432   FYBMH   757  B  0
    1:30P ATL  2:50P O   DL    311   FYBMH   M80     0
    8:49a D   11:57a STL TW    262   FYBQV   M80  B  0
    1:28P STL  4:49P O   TW    450   FYBQV   72S  L/S 0
    9:15a D   12:51P ORD UA    236   FYBMQ   757  B/S 0
    2:43P ORD  6:17P O   UA    428   FYBMQ   72S  S  0
    9:35a D   12:25P DFW DL   1184   FYBMH   M80  S  0
    1:25P DFW  5:00P O   DL    396   FYBMH   L10  L/S 0
   10:45a D    3:51P ATL DL    317   FYBMH   763  L/S 0
    5:06P ATL  6:25P O   DL    869   FYBMH   L10  S  0
   10:45a D    4:09P IAD UA    342   FYBMQ   D10  L  0
    5:20P IAD  7:27P O   UA   1465   FYBMQ   72S  S  0
X56 10:46a D   4:15P IAD UA    688   FYBMQ   757  L  0
D- 5AUG 10:46a D  5:20P IAD UA  688  FYBMQ   72S  D  0
    5:20P IAD  7:27P O   UA   1465   FYBMQ   72S  S  0
   10:46a D    4:15P IAD UA    688   FYBMQ   757  L  0
```

To Honolulu from Denver:

```
To HONOLULU, OAHU; HAWAII    HST HNL

    5:15P STL  8:40P O   TW    264   FYBQV   72S  D  0
    1:20P D    4:15P DFW DL    260   FYBMH   M80  L/S 0
    5:12P DFW  8:45P O   DL    452   FYBMH   767  D  0
    2:40P D    7:28P ATL DL    804   FYBMH   757  S  0
    8:24P ATL  9:45P O   TW    747   FYBQV   72S  S  0
    2:40P D    7:28P ATL DL    804   FYBMH   757  S  0
    8:54P ATL 10:10P O   DL    348   FYBMH   L10     0
    4:16P D    7:31P STL TW     88   FYBQV   M80  D  0
    8:15P STL 11:42P O   TW    214   FYBQV   M80     0
X7  5:10P D    9:52P ATL DL    664   FYBMH   757  D  0
   10:46P ATL 11:59P O   DL    163   FYBMH   757     0
```

CAR RENTAL INFORMATION

Car Rental Rates: 5 day minimum; weekend rate; all free/unlimited mileage

	Orlando/Disney World	Honolulu
Economy	$152.99 per week	$145.99 per week
Mid-sized	$258.99 per week	$249.99 per week
Luxury	$299.99 per week	$370.99 per week

DISNEY WORLD ACCOMMODATIONS

✔ ★ **COMFORT INN.** *(Box 22776, Lake Buena Vista 32830) 6442 Palm Pkwy, at Vista Ctr.* 407/239-7300; FAX 407/239-7740. 640 rms, 5 story. Feb–mid-Apr, June–Aug: S, D up to 4, $69; family rates; lower rates rest of yr. Crib free. TV. 2 pools, 1 heated. Cafe 6:30–10:30 am, 6–9 pm. Bar 5:30 pm–2 am. Ck-out 11 am. Coin lndry. Valet serv. Sundries. Gift shop. Free Walt Disney World, Universal Studios transportation. Game rm. Accept cr cds.

★ ★ **HOWARD JOHNSON PARK SQUARE INN AND SUITES.** *(8501 Palm Pkwy, Lake Buena Vista 32830) I-4 exit 27 to FL 535, N to Vista Ctr.* 407/239-6900; FAX 407/239-1287. 308 rms, 3 story, 86 suites. Feb–mid-Apr, June–Aug, late Dec: S, D $97–$110; each addl. $10; suites $140; under 18 free; lower rates rest of yr. Crib $5. TV; in-rm movies. 2 pools, heated; wading pool, whirlpool, poolside serv in season. Playground. Cafe 7–11:30 am, 5–11 pm. Bar 4:30 pm–midnight. Ck-out noon. Coin lndry. Meeting rms. Bellhops. Concierge. Sundries. Gift shop. Airport transportation. Free Walt Disney World transportation. Game rm. Lawn games. Refrigerator in suites; some minibars. Balconies. Landscaped courtyard. Accept cr cds.

★ ★ ★ **HILTON AT WALT DISNEY WORLD VILLAGE.** *(1751 Hotel Plaza Blvd., Lake Buena Vista 32830) In Walt Disney World Village.* 407/827-4000; FAX 407/827-4872. 813 rms, 10 story, 26 suites. Feb–mid-May, late Dec: S, D $155–$230; each addl. $20; suites $470–$705; family rates; lower rates rest of yr. Crib free. TV; cable. 2 pools, 1 heated; wading pool, poolside serv, lifeguard. Playground. Free supervised child's activities. Cafe 6:30–1 am. Bar 11–2 am; entertainment, dancing. Ck-out 11 am. Coin lndry. Convention facilities. Concierge, Barber, beauty shop, Valet parking. Airport transportation. Free Walt Disney World transportation. Lighted tennis, pro. Golf privileges, pro, pro shop, putting green, driving range. Exercise equipt; weight machine, bicycles, whirlpool, sauna. Game rm. Minibars; some bathrm phones, refrigerators. Some private patios, balconies. LUXURY LEVEL: TOWERS. 80 rms, 4 suites, 2 floors. S, D $250; suites $570–$805. Private lounge, honor bar. Wet bar in suites. Complimentary continental bkfst, refreshments. Accept cr cds.

CONFIRMATION SHEET

PASSENGERS			BUS PHONE	AGENT	DATE BOOKED	DATE DEPART	DATE RETURN		CASH PAID OUT		
								DATE	AMOUNT	PAID TO	
			HOME PHONE	BILL TO:							
								CASH RECEIVED			
			BUS PHONE	ADDRESS				DATE	AMOUNT	PAID TO	
			HOME PHONE								

A I R · B U S · H O T E L · A U T O	FROM	TO	CARRIER	FLT	CLASS	DAY DATE	DEPART	ARRIVE	TOTAL COST	DATE	AMOUNT	PAID TO
										NET COMMISSIONS		
	DATE	HOTEL	CITY		NITES	ROOM	PLAN	RATE		DATE	AMOUNT	PAID TO
	DATE	COMPANY	CITY		MAKE-MODEL	DROP OFF-TIME/PLACE		RATE				

BANK TRANSACTION INFORMATION

CURRENCY	*100*	*00*
COIN		

DATE *March 16* 19____

CHECKS AND OTHER ITEMS ARE RECEIVED FOR DEPOSIT SUBJECT TO THE TERMS AND CONDITIONS OF THIS FINANCIAL INSTITUTION'S ACCOUNT AGREEMENT. **DEPOSITS MAY NOT BE AVAILABLE FOR IMMEDIATE WITHDRAWAL.**

_____
SIGN HERE ONLY IF CASH RECEIVED FROM DEPOSIT

**MIDTOWN MUTUAL
SAVINGS BANK**

: 743   000   1 3 002   24

C H E C K S	LIST CHECKS SINGLY	*50*	*00*
		869	*23*
TOTAL FROM OTHER SIDE			
SUB-TOTAL		*1,019*	*23*
TOTAL ITEMS	LESS CASH RECEIVED		
TOTAL DEPOSIT		*1,019*	*23*

ACCOUNT NUMBER *0080420*

3/47-10
BRANCH B

DEPOSIT TICKET

PLEASE ITEMIZE
ADDITIONAL
CHECKS ON
REVERSE
SIDE

Annmarie Welsh-Jones
1476 Park Place
Corvallis, OR 97330
503-555-7372

1258

_____ 19____

Pay to the order of _*Leroy Nelson*_ $ *50.00*
Amount

Fifty and no/100 _____ ~~Dollars~~

FOR _____   *Annmarie Walsh-Jones*
SIGNATURE

G & C Electric
147 E. 49th Street
San Diego, CA 92110

2-10
1903

Pay to the Order of _*Leroy Nelson*_   *869.23*
Amount

Eight hundred sixty-nine and 23/100 _____ Dollars

Payable through: Northern Bank
7 Wall Street
New York, NY 00571

Allen Shih
Comptroller

Balance Sheet							
Time	Cash Bal	A#	With/A	Ty	Dep/A	Ty	Cash Bal
9:30 AM	8000.00						8000.00
9:31		0077412			1846.22	ch	
9:40		0084361	1400.00	c			
9:53		0141233	300.00	c	470.37	ch	
9:59		1004217			789.32	ch	
10:04		0378400	48.95	ch	502.02	c	
10:09		0062417			2317.62	ch	
10:11		0499828			1730.00	c	
10:29		1783692	150.00	c	300.00	ch	
10:35		0023476			4572.36	ch	
10:39		9923476	350.00	c			
10:49		8519540	2000.00	c			
11:16		5549012	350.98	c	5076.39	ch	
11:22		0012874	1357.00	c	17456.00	ch	
11:28		0499662	450.00	c	10598.32	ch	
11:35		9098123			6500.00	c	
11:50		7659901	125.75	c	500.00	ch	
11:58		4466291	250.00	c	950.00	ch	
12:03 PM ROBBERY							

HEAD HOUSEKEEPING SCHEDULE

DATE: _____

Cleaning time
30 minutes/vacated room (v)
15 minutes/occupied room (o)

Staff	Caroline	Tanya	Tuyet	Tatiana	Head Housekeeper
8:30 A.M.					
9:00					
10:00					
11:15	break	break	break	break	break
11:30					
12:30 P.M.	lunch	lunch	lunch	lunch	lunch
1:30					
2:30					
3:45	break	break	break	break	break
4:00					
5:00					
5:30					

RICCAR MODEL 2200

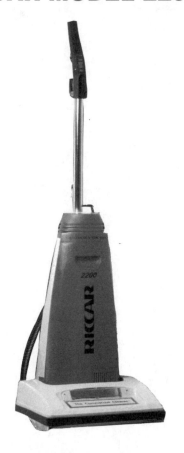

	Model 2200
Clean Air System	Yes
Triple Clean Air Filtration	Yes
Filter Bag Supporter	Yes
Metal Brush Roll	12" Steel, 4 Replaceable Brushes
Bottom Plate	Chrome
3-Position Handle	Yes
Handle	Chrome
Handle Grip	Deluxe
Automatic Carpet Height Adjustment	Yes
Quick, Easy Cord Release	Yes
Edge Cleaning	Yes
Furniture Guard	Yes
Headlight	Yes
Motor	7.8 amp
Cord Length	40 Foot Grounded
Dust Capacity	9 Quart
Carrying Handle	Yes
Dust Bag	C12
Optional Tools	6 Piece - 8 Piece
Weight	15 Pounds
Color	Red and Grey

PANASONIC JET-FLO MC-6217

Specifications		MC-6217
Air Flow		Safe Guard System
Triple Filter System		Yes
Automatic Carpet Height Adjustment		Yes
Three-Position Handle		Yes
Motor (Input Power)		Motor: 720W (Input Power: 7.0A)
Headlight		Yes
Vac Gauge		Yes
Agitator		14" Metal All-Brush
Edge Cleaning		Yes (Right and Left)
Suction Control		Yes
Rug/Floor Selector		Yes
Dust Bag Capacity		10.0 qt.
Cord Length		33 ft.
Weight	Main Body	15.0 lbs.
	Shipping	17.8 lbs.
Carton Cube		2.09 cft.
Color		Light Gray
Belt Type		Panasonic Type UB-2/UB-3